Rasta, Babylon, Jamming

The Music and Culture of Roots Reggae

ROBERT FLEMING

With K Kelly McElroy

Rasta, Babylon, Jamming, *The Music and Culture of Roots Reggae* © 2017 by Robert Fleming.

All rights reserved. Printed in the United States of America. No part of this book may be used or reproduced in any manner whatsoever without written permission except in the case of brief quotations embodied in critical articles or reviews.

This book is a work of non-fiction.

For information contact: info@uptownmediaventures.com
Book and Cover design by Team Uptown

http://uptownmediaventures.com

ISBN: **978-1-68121-060-5**

First Edition: July 2017

10 9 8 7 6 5 4 3 2 1

Dedication

To Will Fleming, my grandfather and adventurer from the island of resistance and rebellion – who refused to let others think for him.

Table of Contents

Foreword — 7

Introduction — 11

Hymns of Jah and Politics — 15

Jamming On The Streets And The Studio — 23

Roots Talk
(Three Personal Interviews of Reggae Greats) — 29

Pivotal Reggae Pioneers — 35

Vintage and Modern Reggae Album Collection — 61

16 Essential Reggae Films — 97

Selected Bibliography — 105

About The Authors — 107

FOREWORD

When Reggae burst on the world stage, its musical radiance was dazzling. It expanded the pantheon of world music greatly, featuring new sounds deeply rooted in history, tradition and the culture of Jamaica, West Indies.

In his new book, *Rasta, Babylon, Jamming: The Music and Culture of Roots Reggae*, Robert Fleming feeds the flame ignited in the 1970s by the sonar outlaws Jimmy Cliff, Burning Spear, Peter Tosh, Bob Marley and the Wailers, and others.

Reggae is a music that reinvigorated the soul force of world music. Reggae is about love, redemption, resistance, empowerment and salvation. It's a music that speaks clearly and boldly against the evils of colonialism, capitalism and social injustice.

In "Hymns of Jah and Politics" and "Jamming On the Streets and In The Studio," Fleming tells us how he discovered Reggae and how it affected him with its rhythms and themes. He explains the evolution of roots Reggae and the motley crew of producers who shaped the music. We get a peek into the minds of the music's creators through their own words in the latter chapter, several of them resisting the allure of profits over protest.

This book traces the development of Reggae, a swift history in the making, though a fractious one. Its many facets dazzle even as they crossed all boundaries – politics, religious suppression and exaltation, and poverty. These things are all part of the soil in which the roots of Reggae grew.

We are guided through the maze of causes and effects and given the historical context that informs Jamaican life and culture even to this day. A deep and profound history of resistance to enslavement, colonialism and oppression has long been an essential part of the Jamaican character. We see how Jamaica evolved from the distant past to the present and how all the links make the great chain, from Pan- Africanist Garvey to mega star musician Bob Marley, among others.

Reggae's international reverberation energizes all the realms of consciousness that it seeks to combine: the physical pleasure of dance and movement; the sensuality of the beat; the spirit of resistance in the way it rebukes oppression; and spirituality in its avowal of resilience and transcendence.

Reggae affirms what the best in the strengths of indigenous and folk tradition, defining the promise of hope and faith in the life situation of hearts and souls, struggles and goals.

Rasta, Babylon, Jamming

This is a journey for self-knowledge and identity. In many ways, the music, characterized as laid back and imitated from Ithaca to Ireland, has a legacy of bloodshed and internal struggle staining its grooves. Although Reggae most often calls for peace and harmony, there was a tradition of violence surrounding its conception and inception. In this book, we are led surefooted through that unpleasant part of the story.

The international seeding is another interesting aspect of the Reggae's history – both England and America figure in Reggae's inception and commercialization.

As a child of the Caribbean and the granddaughter of four Garveyites, this journey resonates deeply for me. The extensive record collection of my hip parents, predominated by jazz, included songs my brother and I would learn by singing along with my father – Calypso, it was called. Calypso, folk songs performed in Jamaica and Trinidad, soon spread throughout the Caribbean. Our father taught us the lyrics to popular ditties such as "*Mama Look a Boo-boo*" and "*Man Smart but Woman Smarter*." I remember the songs of Mighty Sparrow and Harry Belafonte, as our favorite child-love vinyl sides. We yodeled "*Day-O*" and felt a twinge of longing with the island musical tribute, "*Jamaica Farewell*." We trilled the catchy refrain, "*She Can't Crossover*."

I didn't think of this saucy up-tempo, dance around-and-laugh music as being from the same source as my Blue Mountain grandmother's soothe songs - comfort tunes like "*If I had the Wings of a Dove*," not sung in her Anglican church next store, but with a spiritual feeling nonetheless. Through this book, I understand the connection and progression of the blend of the secular and the spiritual.

My grandfather took my brother and I "home" during the summer of 1965. It was a startling revelation. We were "over the moon" to go to where he was from – especially as many of our classmates went home every summer to the south of the United States.

We saw where he came from, a voluminous home in the Blue Mountains where the dark floors gleamed from being polished with coconut brushes. There were chickens and a family graveyard, a wide wrap-around veranda and the stunning views of mist in the valley each morning and high green hills. It was a stark contrast to Harlem streets of hard concrete that he'd mastered and down the hillside was a town. In that town, we heard the music: our now departed grandmother's songs.

We laughed with recognition and delight. This foreign country was familiar, we wore it like skin. Though born and raised in New York City, we felt the joy of return in the sound, in the cuisine, in the very steam and release of the air. We loved Jamaica.

And that music heard in the little town in St. Anne's Parish would follow and find us, a few short years later, in America. That music would be called Reggae. The world would reverberate with the sounds of struggle and triumph, joy and redemption, hunger and fulfillment, sweat and exhilaration, from that wonderful island.

This is a critical time to examine this music's history. We are invited to appreciate and reflect on it — at a time when so many foundations are under threat, when cultures are being unraveled, subsumed and compromised.

It is a delight to be reminded of those whose sounds once moved us: Judy Mowatt and Sister Carol, Black Uhuru, and Third World, as well as learn about other seminal contributors. It's a kick to make this tour with visual aids, the forgone art of album covers provides another kind of insight as we survey the past. Through the creative eye of K. Kelly McElroy, we are treated with delicious art in the chapters: "Pivotal Reggae Pioneers," "Vintage and Modern Reggae Album Collection," and "16 Essential Reggae Films."

A people without history are doomed. We must be reminded that we can be both entertained and strengthened in our resolve and need to "get up stand up, stand up for our rights" as assuredly as we can celebrate 'one love.'

Enjoy the journey into this transforming music.

Akua Lezli Hope
New York, 2017

INTRODUCTION

"I grew up economically poor, spiritually rich. Even though
I had this condition, that kind of balance made me always
take the downside and put an up to it."

- Jimmy Cliff

This book, *Rasta, Babylon, Jamming: The Music and Culture of Roots Reggae*, has been a long time in coming. Sometimes an idea takes years, even decades, before it bears fruit.

When I was in my early 20s, I was sitting in a small apartment near Kinsman Avenue on the West Side of Cleveland, Ohio, being schooled by a musician on the artistry of the jazz piano. My friend loved all of the jazz cats on the ivories: Art Tatum, Bud Powell, Monk, Count Basie, Mal Waldron, Wynton Kelly, McCoy Tyner, Cecil Taylor, and the Grand Wizard of the keys – Duke Ellington. I was a listener of jazz since junior high. I spent my paper route money on Bebop and free jazz at the dime store.

It was the start of the 1970s. A local music publication had just hired me as a writer to interview performers in all of the genres and to review albums. Willard Jenkins, a veteran of the magazine, recommended me for the spot. I was determined to do well.

Anyway, returning to the visit to the pianist, he walked among the shelves of the albums, and one disc caught my eye with its gaudy cover. It was the soundtrack of a Jimmy Cliff soundtrack to the movie, *The Harder They Come*. He loaned the record to me and I was mesmerized by the drive and soul of the music. At first, Jimmy Cliff was the man!

There was something more real to his music than I was hearing on the radio. Love songs didn't cut it during this wicked time of Nixon.

In 1974, I convinced the magazine's editors that we needed to talk to Cliff and the reggae was the next big thing. Cliff was touring the States, eager to get new converts. We talked about his new albums, *Struggling Man* and *House of Exile*, and his role as the Jamaican outlaw in the film, *The Harder They Come*. He spoke about the untimely death of his mentor, Leslie Kong, an event that saddened him. But his eyes lit up as the conversation turned to reggae, the poverty, the rude boys, the competition between the studios, the hopelessness of the island's many disenfranchised and voiceless.

Cliff was not the last of the Jamaican musicians that my work discovered amid the flood of music coming my way. Among the titans of the roots reggae featured through the years were: Toots Hibbert, Linton Kwesi Johnson, and the international symbol of the sound – Bob Marley. There were so many others which I cannot recall.

"What your music here has lost is its force, its political power, its love for the poor and hungry," Marley said in an interview on his last tour to the States. "Many of the musicians in Jamaica sing about the struggle. Not so here. The truth has drained out of the sounds here."

The origins of the book happened then and there. Jamaica. I knew my grandfather came from there, a seaman transplanted to the Deep South where he met my grandmother in New Orleans and settled in Mississippi. The white folks there assaulted his wife, brutally beat him, put his eye out, and stole his land. My curiosity was peaked about the history and culture of the island because of this. Now, there was the bold words of Cliff. This music was in my blood.

I proposed the idea for this book to publishers in the late 1970's. It was too soon. Whenever reggae performers came to Cleveland and New York, I interviewed them. Although the audiences were mainly white, I learned the rich tradition of the music from the entertainers. What I loved about the spirit of reggae was the bands and singers never gave their fans less than their maximum effort. The other thing was the music's very hardcore political and spiritual message. It was the modern music of former slaves in revolt, a mix of soul and cultural pride with the bite of agitation and self-determination. It knocked me on my ass.

Also, at a time when the kids were reading Iceberg Slim and Donald Goines and getting enraged by the failed War on Drugs, the music somehow fit more than Motown and Gamble and Huff. In my neighborhood, there was much toxicity, an abundance of cruelty, bad intentions, rage, envy, suspicions and gun violence. Later, Jimmy Cliff and Bob Marley would tell me it was the same in Trench Town and other depressed areas in Jamaica, the same ailments, the same torments.

Rather than the moral problems posed by some of the current gangsta rap crew, reggae is about love, redemption, empowerment, and salvation. Several critics point the modern tunes breeds the attitude which makes the young sick and perverted. Society pointed at the horde of poor black youth, confused, frustrated, dehumanized, and feeling outside of the majority white society. However, reggae celebrates the positive anthems of Marvin Gaye, James Brown, Sly Stone, and Curtis Mayfield. It celebrates a victory over self-hatred, self-destruction, and violence against the community.

When I took this book idea to mainstream publishers, they didn't want any part of a music that spoke against colonialism, capitalism, or social injustice. Other than the scourge of the ganja trade, they complained the music of these blackheart men and women would fall flat with the soul experience of Black America or even the protest politics of the Hood. I disagreed with that assertion.

I viewed the book as a transcendent resource book, capable of enlightening, informing and providing a point of entry into one of the world's political, spiritual, and musical cultures. Furthermore, a key contribution to the book would be the musical legacy of Rastafarians, the songs of freedom and pride, the adoration of the lives of the visionary Marcus Garvey and Haile Selassie I, who the Rasta believe to be descended from King Solomon. Also, the information about the singers and musicians and producers will support the essential Afrocentric message and the Rasta doctrine of resistance, political self-determination and Black survival.

Marcus Garvey, the controversial icon of Rastafarianism and reggae, honored Black consciousness and race pride. "The Black skin is not a badge of shame, but rather a glorious symbol of national greatness," he proclaimed to his followers before he was harassed by the U.S. government.

Along with the additional list of critical reggae films, I explored the nuances of roots reggae as the most popular Jamaican music export, evolving from mento through soul, ska, dub, and dancehall. Like Motown's Barry Gordy, the Jamaican Sound owes its collective clout throughout the world to its innovative producers such as Leslie Kong, Clancy Eccles, Joe Gibbs, Keith Hudson, Chris Blackwell, Lee "Scratch" Perry Karl Patterson, Sonia Pottinger and King Jammy. Collectively, they wrote and produced music designed to praise fun and good times, and to promote healing and loving in our communities.

A bonus in the book is the collection of vintage and modern album covers, rendering this edition a keepsake and a collector's item. This is reggae at its best with no gimmicks, pure and unadulterated. This is reggae that seeks to capture the attention of the world, one listener at a time. This is reggae that belongs to everybody.

Robert Fleming
October, 2016
New York City

Hymns of Jah and Politics

"We are going to emancipate ourselves from mental slavery, because whilst others might free the body, none but ourselves can free the mind."

- Marcus Garvey (1937)

Needless to say, the Rastafarian faith fueled the energy and power of reggae. Its cultural and political influence resisted all efforts to contain it by short-sighted men who thought it could be manipulated and exploited for economic gain or class advantage.

The origins of the faith go back to the suffering and torment of the misery of some 30 million Africans taken from their homeland. Bands of white slavers and their backers stole thousands of Ibos from lower Niger, Mandingos and Hausas from the Ivory and Gold Coasts, and others for the thriving agricultural markets in North America and the Caribbean.

Slave resistance on the island was fierce, aggressive, and cunning against the slaveholders who used every tactic to bring the imported help under control. Many lives were lost, several plantations razed, in a fever of bloodshed and death. The tradition of protest can be traced to the Maroons, the tribe of courageous slaves in the 17th Century, who sought refuge from the oppressors in the mountains. They raised so much hell that the British surrendered to their wishes and signed a peace treaty with them in 1738.

The oppressed felt the English didn't keep their word. Throughout the island, they rose up and made their rage felt. Two important revolts against the status quo turned the tide: the 1831 Sam Sharpe Rebellion and the 1865 Morant Bay Rebellion. The slaves were outraged with their employers did not live up to the royal agreement. It was business as usual for the whites but the situation was changing.

Slavery ended in Jamaica in 1838, but the lash of the colonial whip and degrading shackle has remained with the residents of the island to the present day.

The old guard and the business elite saw there was a transformation among the locals, because they wanted something closer to their reality. Even the dismayed Christian missionaries noticed it. There was a rejection of common worship practices of priests of Christ in preference to the African traditional rituals. Historians have termed this trend, The Great Revival, the spiritual reversal of two different faiths from 1860-1861.

By the early 1900s, Pan-African communities sprung up throughout the island. It was in the countryside that Marcus Garvey, the son of a stonemason, emerged from obscurity to become one of the most exciting figures in black history. Born in 1887 in the parish of St. Ann, he was a dynamic young man who wanted a better life for himself and the others he saw around him. He arrived in the U.S. in 1916 and quickly founded the United Negro Improvement Association (UNIA), an organization created for economic self-reliance, race pride, and repatriation for blacks to Africa.

"The Black skin is not a badge of shame, but rather a glorious symbol of national greatness," Garvey said to the crowds who followed him on his many tours throughout the country.

Some said Garvey was a con man and a charlatan, but others saw him as a prophet and visionary.

With remarkable business acumen, he organized a newspaper, The Negro World, which prospered in black communities. Also, he launched a steamship, the Black Star Line, in preparation to ferry the many Garveyites back to the African homeland. His sermons preached the potential of black economic freedom, sparking thousands of projects and businesses in the Jim Crow-separated neighborhoods.

"One God! One Aim! One Destiny!" proclaimed Garvey to his thousands of members in the U.S., Central America, and black communities in the Caribbean and Europe.

His aggressive stance on race, politics, and cultural progress earned Garvey enemies on all fronts. The leader's independent attitude dismayed American law officials, namely FBI director J. Edgar Hoover. Hoover, annoyed with the potential of another effective black spokesman, placed agents in Garvey's organization, disrupting it from the inside, giving the Bureau access to every move of the UNIA agenda.

Garvey, ever to seek new alliances, began to explore other options. The NAACP were angered by his meeting with KKK officials to plan sending blacks back to Africa. Hoover was delighted by the isolation of Garvey's UNIA by various civil rights groups, who termed the organization as "misguided" and "confused."

In the manner befitting Garvey's new rating as Public Enemy #1, the domino theory was in full effect, his businesses failed, his supporters harassed, his properties in ligation. In 1922, Garvey and many of the UNIA leadership were jailed and charged with mail fraud. That next year, he received a five year sentence.

American law officials did not want Garvey to die behind bars, causing the masses to consider the leader a martyr. Citing his collection of health issues such as lung ailments and heart disease, he was pardoned by President Calvin Coolidge and deported in 1927.

Before a throng in Kingston that same year, Garvey proclaimed the arrival of a new black messiah: "Look to Africa where a black king shall be crowned, for the day of deliverance is here!"

As Garvey struggled to fend off the Federal witch hunt, his attention was not focused on Africa to see the rise of the new powerful black king ascend to the international stage. In 1935, Garvey went to England after harassment from authorities and surviving a stroke. While recovering, the media played a role in Garvey's decline by publishing a premature obit on June 9, 1940, shocking him severely. Some say that death notice caused his demise from a massive stroke the next day. Garvey was dead at 53.

His body was flown from England in 1964 and returned to Jamaica, where he was named a national hero and a Rasta icon. Crowds flocked to his final resting place to pay him homage, acknowledging the cultural and political contributions of the son of the rural stonemason.

The prophesy of Garvey was manifested in 1930 when a warlord from Ethiopia, Ras Tafari Makonnen, who was crowned the 111th Emperor of Ethiopia, the reputed descendant of King Solomon, the King of Kings, the Lord of Lords. The anointed man assumed the title, Haile Selassie, and the world took notice.

Jamaica got word as the leading publication, *The Daily Gleaner*, announced the newly crowned African king. The believers consulted their Bibles and saw the verses of Revelations 5:5, noting the arrival of the Deliverer: "And one of the elders saith unto me, 'Weep not: behold, the Lion of Judah, the Root of David, hath prevailed to open the Book, and to loose the Seven Seals of God thereof…"

However, the Rasta community combined the holy presence of Selassie with the separatist, nationalist concepts of Garvey to increase their membership during the 1930s. Despite the Great Depression occurring at that time, they embraced the nations of black pride, separatism, self-help, community outreach, and most of all, repatriation of Africa.

Jamaican authorities kept an eye on three leaders of the Rasta movement: Leonard P. Howell, Alexander Bedward, and Joseph Hibbert. They preached the value of black pride and economic independence, with barbed commentary on colonialism and racism. A series of police crackdowns and raids in the 1930s against Rasta enclaves put a target on the followers of the Lion of Judah.

With the crushing failure of Garvey under the might of American capitalism and legality, local politicians sized up the Rastas as "criminal, violent, unclean, lazy, anti-social, and mentally incompetent."

The most courageous of the Rasta spokesmen, Leonard Howell, thumbed his nose in the faces of the authorities by selling portraits of Haile Selassie. He voiced angry anti-colonial statements, drawing more converts to his group. Police singled him out, charging him with sedition, sentencing him to two years in an asylum. However, a well-publicized raid at his Pinnacle commune stirred Rasta enlistment.

The political leaders panicked when workers seized a plantation on the 100th anniversary of Jamaican emancipation on January, 1938, with some loss of life. Suddenly, strikes, marches, revolts and gun battles sprung up all over the island. Irate workers controlled entire areas of the nation. Docks were idle. The police retreated from the wrath of the opposition and the army called into the fray. Still, after the widespread mayhem, new labor regulations were instituted and trade unions legalized.

Howell was released from custody in 1940 and bought a sanctuary in the mountains with 1,500 followers. Dreadlocks appeared in 1947. Ganja was their cash crop. After the 1938 uprising, ganja was put on the national Dangerous Drugs Act, so Howell's Pinnacle camp was raided repeatedly because of allegedly illegal drugs being grown on the premises. In 1954, cops shut the camp down and many followers relocated into Kingston or further into the countryside.

Howell was arrested after the raid in 1960, placed in an asylum. He was labeled insane. Later, he died out of the limelight in 1981.

In the Rasta doctrine, ganja was used in ritualized smoking by the group, prime marijuana in cigar-sized spliffs or communal chalices. The Rastas employed the ganja as a mode for meditation, to unite body and spirit.

Meanwhile, there was a movement to the end of British colonial rule, with two leading local political organizations, People's National Party and its rival, the Jamaican Labour Party. Finally, the British granted the island independence in 1962, with their black, gold, and green flag. However, the army and Rastas fought in a savage battle, with buildings burning, many jailed, and eight dead.

The new government took measures to curtail further political agitation by denying any black American civil rights leaders. However, it permitted a visit of Haile Selassie to Kingston in April 21, 1966, and a huge crowd of over 100,000 Rasta faithful surrounded his airplane.

More lined the route of the motorcade in this blessed day for the followers of Selassie. They mourned when he later died in a small room in Addis Ababa in 1975 after an army coup.

Significantly, the mix of politics and music was quite evident in the origins of the modern political and cultural organizations. Going back to the past of Jamaica in the last century, William Alexander Bustamante, a progressive leader, created the Bustamante Industrial Trade Union (BITU), the first trade union in the Caribbean. His cousin, Norman Washington Manley, a lawyer and Harvard-educated Rhodes scholar, established the nation's first political party, the People's National Party (PNP).

A few years later, Bustamante was jailed and his cousin obtained his release, but there was an ideological split between them. In 1943, Bustamante quit Manley's organization and formed a rival group, the Jamaica Labour Party (JLP).

The push for independence was ongoing. When Manley's PNP assumed control in 1955, it worked to free the country from British's rigid grip. When the British offered to include Jamaica in the West Indies Federation, a 1961 proposal to unify its colonial activities in the Caribbean, the island refused the invitation in a heated referendum.

It was during that campaign where Bustamante's JLP used the Clancy Eccles' song, "Freedom," to turn the votes against the Federation. Ironically, the Eccles song is a prideful song with a Rasta theme, the first instance where popular music was used in a national political campaign. However, Bustamante later turned on the Rastas in a wave of police crackdowns.

Music also played a role in the career of Edward Seaga, who formed an early Jamaica label, West Indies Records Limited (WIRL), in 1956. He became a JLP government minister in the early 1960s and later became the island's prime minister in 1980. Throughout the career, he used popular music in his JLP campaigns and the PNP countered a similar strategy, a tit-for-tat musical chess game.

In 1968, the Ethiopians released "Everything Crash," a song about the suffering of the dispossessed, which was banned by Prime Minister Hugh Shearer of JLP. The Rastas called Shearer "Pharoah," the beleaguered Egyptian ruler with a downtrodden people in captivity. When Michael Manley, the son of the PNP founder, decided to run against Shearer, the Rastas named him Joshua after the Biblical figure, a coveted title since he had recently visited Ethiopia. Haile Selassie gave him a staff, termed the "Rod of Correction."

As the 1971 campaign continued, the Rasta community embraced Manley's socialist policies, penning songs to ensure him a victory. Singer Delroy Wilson's 1971 hit, "Better Must Come" became his theme song. Summing up the candidates of the election, Junior Byles released two singles in 1972, "Joshua's Desire" and "Pharoah Hiding."

Knowing the impact of music on the masses, Manley created the PNP Musical Bandwagon, a flatbed truck with a stage, including talents as Bob Marley, Inner Circle, Alton Ellis, Dennis Brown and Judy Mowatt. The clever Manley incorporated many Rasta themes in his stump speeches, winning over the poor, middle class, and intellectual elite with his anti-colonial and anti-capitalist slogans.

Manley, enjoying the landslide win, wanted to improve the plight of poor, but the American phobia about communism and Cuba crippled his efforts. Castro was off-limits. Secretary of State Henry Kissinger threatened Manley to dismantle a billion-dollar trade deal with Jamaica if Manley continued to support Cuba in his Angola proxy war. The 1973 oil crisis forced the island to borrow expensive loans from the International Monetary Fund (IMF), but the debts only subverted Jamaica's economy and turned the people against Manley.

Still, Manley tried to get his programs into production. The Rastas found themselves in disfavor, with their dreadlocks and Jah worship. Dread acts were prohibited from clubs and dancehalls. Even Rasta musicians were discarded from established band.

Media, sympathetic to the JLP cause, brought up an obscure ancient report on the Rastas, stating: "…the cult was not likely to attract intellectuals, the majority of their members with low mentality, and apart from encouraging wayward youths to smoke ganja and creating minor disturbances, the Rastafarians have no real influence on the communities in which they live."

But Western publications took notice of the Rasta Community, examining their customs and culture. From their belief in the Old Testament to their dreadlocks and ganja rituals, the foreign writers looked with favor on their Ital (natural) diet based on vegetables, their disdain of additives on food, no meat, no alcohol or coffee or milk. The government didn't like that they paid no taxes or regular employment.

For some reason, shipments of illegal guns appeared in the poor areas, the squatter towns and slums. Some said CIA was behind the rise of violence. As one official said, there were certain areas on the island where you put your life in danger if you went for a walk. The murder rate tripled as police lost control of heavily armed thugs preying on the poor.

Manley was losing control of his country. With U.S. support, Seaga asked Manley to declare a state of emergency as the political violence increased. In 1976, JLP gangs attacked Trench Town, a poor part of Kingston, and a gun battle ensued, followed by the torching of homes and bodies in the streets. Some of the classic reggae albums reflected the suffering, hopelessness, and crime in Jamaica, such as Bob Marley and the Wailers, Burning Spear, Inner Circle, the Congos, Dennis Brown and Aswad.

Also, there was an assassination attempt on Bob Marley in December, 1976 by persons unknown, possibly JLP operatives. Friends were afraid for the singer's life. He promptly left the island, going to London where he recorded his latest album, *Exodus*. One song,

"Ambush," let the world know Marley felt about the current situation in his country:

> "See them fighting for power, but they know not the hours
> So they bribe dem with their guns, cars and money
> Trying to belittle our integrity.

> They say what we know is just what they teach us
> We're so ignorant 'cos every time they can reach us
> Through political strategy, they keep us hungry…"

The political chaos reached a peak when a PNP protest was attacked by armed JLP members, resulting in dozens killed and four cops. Another incident occurred when a JLP arson squad burned a huge area of a West Kingston slum, leaving over 500 people homeless. Manley stressed harsher penalties for the escalating violence, long sentences for those caught with guns. A state of emergency was declared by the Jamaican leadership.

A hit by Junior Byles, "When Will Better come," kept playing on the radio. He had been an ardent supporter of Manley and his party, but now he was disappointed like so many other Rastas. After the 1974 death of Selassie, the singer withdrew into silence and made only one more album.

Bob Marley, now recovered, later returned home and put on the seminal 1978 "One Love Peace" concert in Kingston, bringing together Manley and Seaga onstage, hoping for redemption and conciliation. There was a historic photo of Marley embracing the two men. However, conditions worsened on the island with open violence between the political parties.

"Politics affects our lives a lot in Jamaica, because it's such a small country with so few people that whatever gets decided is felt more or less straight away," said Jimmy Cliff. "Moods travel the country so quickly because there's not many ways to avoid what's going on. Or so it goes for the poor people - it's only the rich that can afford to isolate themselves from politics and not be affected by governmental changes in the country. But as it is the poor people who makes most of the good music, it's they that have a big say."

In 1980, the conservative Seaga government won and repealed all of the socialist gains of Manley. Along with a new pro-capitalism strategy, the island turned from ganja to cocaine consumption, with violent cartels and gangs roaming the slums. Not long after that, Bob Marley died of cancer, ending the Gold Age of reggae.

Jamming On the Streets and the Studio

"Reggae is a music of power. Reggae is meant to change the system."

- Joe Higgs, star producer

Sound, the collective sound of Jamaican music. It was the sound that allowed the joy of dancing, the passion of love, the curative power of healing.

From the chill of the political Cold War and the rush of liberation for former colonial lands, that sound permitted the downtrodden and voiceless to secure a sense of self, to step out culturally into the larger world, and make a statement in a sterile environment that resisted them.

The listening experience of the constantly evolving Jamaican sound fit perfectly in the timeline of the citizens of color throwing off the British yoke. It made them feel human. It celebrated life. It celebrated emotional, cultural, political independence but with some complexities and complications.

Still, the sound of the people of color served notice to the musical establishment that it possessed energy and verve without going to the conservatory. It refused to be anything other than itself. It was not phony.

A quote by the late Dr. Oliver Sacks, the author of the 2007 *Musicophilia: Tales of Music and the Brain,* immediately came to mind. "One does not need to have any formal knowledge of music, nor, indeed, to be particularly "musical" – to enjoy music and to respond to it at the deepest levels," he said. "Music is part of being human and there is no human culture in which it is not highly developed and esteemed."

Now, imagine the Jamaican sound in the early 50s and 60s that was molded by a few musical pioneers. Like the golden age of African-American R & B and soul music that bloomed regionally in Detroit, Memphis, Chicago, Philadelphia, New York and other areas, the early producers steered the sound into commercial profit, seizing control of the interest of the young in the clubs, dancehall, and street parties.

From the start, the producers challenged the sound system trend by auditioning the singers and bands in that chaotic world. A hellish litmus test. They felt that the applause, coupled with insults and ridicule, were good training for rejection. These talent scouts were businessmen above all, obsessed with making money from their product, and at the same time, competing with each other.

Where the sound systems made imported American R&B popular throughout the 1950s, a group of important producers became known to the Jamaican listeners on Kingston's "Beat Street" in the 1960s, including Duke Reid, Sir Coxsone Dodd, and King Edwards. Rivalries arose between the various styles, including violence, gunplay, and fist fights at the dancehalls. The major colorful character in this gathering was the flamboyant Duke Reid, called the "King of Sounds and Blues," who was formerly a cop and always wore his .45 in his waist. He surrounded himself with some tough thugs loyal to him. A rival said Reid was sometimes carried to big events on a throne, with a crown and flowing cape.

Reid's major opposition, Sir Coxsone, was younger, stylish, and the gift of gab. He often visited the States, bringing back music, especially jazz. Reid tried to harass and intimidate his rival, but to no avail. His style, the Coxsone Downbeat, became very popular with musicians and listeners alike. It attracted many star talents, including Lee "Scratch" Perry and Prince Buster and soon folks were hopping and twisting to the beat at many spots, even at the Silver Dollar whorehouse on Hanover St. Also, under the influence of Coxsone, other performers such as Count Machuki, Red Hopeton and King Stitt.

"Duke Reid the Trojan had the sound of the day," Count Machuki said. "He had the strength of money and equipment. But Coxsone had the records, talent, and exclusive selecting."

The legendary guitarist Ernie Ranglin, the musical arranger for most of the Coxsone productions, summed up the essence of the Jamaican sound: "It was ghetto music and in Jamaica they used to put that music…This music was a rebel music even then, the way society looked at and at themselves, they treated it like was against the idea of society. It was like we were the outcasts who played that music."

Quickly becoming a major player, Prince Buster learned his craft from Coxsone. He scored a big ska hit, "Ten Commandments" in the 60s, and while his music was closely linked to ska, most of his chart toppers were in the rocksteady fashion, including "Judge Dread" and "Ghost Dance." The musician-producer toured England regularly, building a loyal audience, and some said he brought the house down on the popular British TV pop show, *Ready, Steady, Go!* in a way that the kiddies only thought the Who, Stones, or the Byrds could do. Once he turned to producing, he was involved in the total recording process, with a very keen eye for artistry and presentation.

And there was Vincent "King" Edwards, who came from the country and carved a niche in Jamaica's music legacy. He tried to crush the sound system scene of the Yankee R&B imports by offering an alternative to the Reid-Coxsone monopoly, but failed. He peaked in the early 1960s, produced records until 1964, then quitting to enter politics.

King Edwards, a fairly conservative man, got out of the scene when the dancehalls became violent and the rowdy performers valued a good time, smoking and carousing, over the quality of entertainment. "Then you find the studio was totally full of smoke. You have to be a smoker in the studio.

So I asked my brother to deal with that aspect. But he was too much of a businessman, so we didn't do much there. But Duke Reid and Coxsone did well."

Although the rivalry between Reid and Coxsone could get deadly when the followers of both camps tangled in sporadic violence, time healed that deep wound as the two music titans allowed their long-standing spat behind them and made up before Duke Reid died.

Yes, it was the time of the producer as artist. The music was moving so fast, jumping from one style to another, moving through one trend into something else. Around the country, studios were popping up. Some businessmen tried the music game, but quickly exited. Others signed up singers and bands, renting small spaces for their equipment, or arrogantly leasing larger studios when they thought they had a sure thing. Loyalty was forgotten as many performers hopped from producer to producer, from studio to studio.

There were other players on the constantly evolving music scene: Ken Khouri's Federal studio, the Tuari family's Caribbean Records, as well as the contributions of Leslie Kong, Vincent Chin, Lindon Pottinger, Joe Gibbs, Bunny Lee, and Winston Lowe.

Needless to say, the big producers made bold and reckless moves, often gambling on new talent. The competition was fierce, and there were many casualties. Very few singers or musicians made any real money, with some barely able to survive.

However, most of the producers strived for quality and innovation in the "Jamaican Sound." Other than the live venues, they had to fight to have the music heard, especially when the ska and rocksteady began to transform into an even more political, activist sound. The ska producers from the Kingston studios turned out rocking instrumentals from 1965 to 1967, much to the delight of a Jamaican market that thrived on anything that let them forget the grinding poverty surrounding them.

At the end of the 1960s, the producers pursued a series of significant stylistic shifts, moving from the dancing rifts and band instrumentals of ska and rocksteady to the emerging signature rhythms of reggae. The radio stations first resisted this sound and the early reggae listeners stayed up past midnight to enjoy the anti-colonial, anti-capitalism rhythms and lyrics by what some called "the tribe of blackheart men."

A younger group of musician-producers tapped into the rage and disillusionment of the poorest of the poor, shaping their product with an urgent sense of quality and innovation. One of the major creators of the new sound was Lee "Scratch" Perry, a former teen dancing champ, who went to seek work for Duke Reid, but the producer's insulting manner led him to go to the man's rival. By 1959, he became Coxsone's A&R man, signing new talent and recording a modest hit, "Chicken Scratch." He left Studio One in 1966 due to a lack of royalties, launched Upsetter Records, and had a success, "Return To Django" three years later.

Perry enjoyed overwhelming popularity among performers during the late 1960s to the late 1970s, working over 60 albums and a total of nearly 400 singles as a solo act and producer. He collaborated with Joe Gibbs as a producer, working with the Wailers, U-Roy, Junior Byles, Errol Brown, the Heptones, Prince Jazzbo, Vin Gordon, the Pioneers, and the Congos.

"I expect artists to do exactly as I say," Perry said. "I teach them everything. How to play. How to move, everything. I am a dictator."

A sound wizard in the world of dub, Perry teamed with the highly creative King Tubby, the master of the remix. In fact, the team released one of the first dub albums, "Blackboard Jungle Dub" (1973). Some musicians praised King Tubby as the perfect sound engineer, with the skill to enhance the soul and energy of a song. With an uncanny talent for merging sounds, he, the engineer as auteur, worked his magic on tapes provided by producers.

One artist, Dave Barker, produced by Perry, didn't mince words about the strict producer: "He was totally nuts. When he was mixing, nobody goes near the studio. He's lock himself in. He doesn't answer the phone."

When Perry opened the influential Black Ark studio in the 1970s, the popularity of his artists further solidified his reputation, bringing several of his acts to global fame. That allowed him to sign a 1976 licensing deal with Island Records. Many critics believed Perry was a victim of his success, extending himself too far financially.

The fortunes of so many producers rose and fell during the golden age of modern Jamaican music. Nobody was as visible as Chris Blackwell, founder of Island Records. Probably this fame was because of his management was so closely tied to the meteoric rise of Bob Marley and the Wailers and the worldwide fame of several acts under his label.

An enterprising youth, Blackwell formed Island Records at age 22 in 1959, and produced a hit, Laurel Aithen's "Boogie In My Bones," which stayed on the charts at number one for 13 weeks. He returned to England in 1962 where he sold records out of his car to the Jamaican community. Many of the reggae artists said he stiffed them but others believed he was a shrewd businessman who could get them publicity on the world stage.

"The bigger labels are supermarkets," Blackwell said. "I like to think of Island as a very classy delicatessen."

If you look at Island's track records from the 1960s to 1980s, you'll see what Blackwell meant: Bob Marley & The Wailers, Sly & Robbie, Toots & The Maytals, Third World, Nirvana, King Crimson, Traffic, Cat Stevens, Robert Palmer, Roxy Music, and Grace Jones.

Of Marley, the largest reggae export, Blackwell commented: "He trusted my instincts, which were that he should go after being a rock star, rather than a star on black American radio. His music was rough and raw and exciting but all black American music at the time other than James Brown was very slick and smooth. Bob trusted me on that, he was as keen as I was."

From the reggae's golden age, Blackwell's reach went far beyond rock or the Jamaican music product. He formed Mango Records to showcase several stellar world musical talent, including Burning Spear, Black Uhuru, Baaba Maal, Salif Keita, Third World, Angelique Kidjo, and King Sunny Ade. Following changing musical trends, Blackwell sold his stake in Island in 1989 and finally quit the company in 1997.

When reggae reached its peak and the rapid ground swell of hip-hop music moving through the State and England, some of the faithful fans of the roots trend remained but others fled for the gangsta sound. The local producers knew the listeners could be fickle, first following one sound, then the other. Music critics would tell you that the genuine reggae product was still be recorded and sold on the island, but the global market was no longer there.

What happened to reggae was the big money men, like Blackwell and Virgin's Richard Branson, saw the music as strictly profit. It was true that British record companies exploited Jamaican artists and studios, milking them dry. At the conclusion of the 1970s and early 1980s, so much music was being pumped out, forming a glut.

Roots reggae, as we knew it, limped along but died a glorious death. For those who were fans, it will always live in our collective memories and fill our homes.

Roots Talk

(Three Personal Interviews of Reggae Greats by Robert Fleming)

Jimmy Cliff: Reggae's Ambassador –at-Large

In his early teens, Jimmy Cliff left his small village to go to Kingston and soon had his first hit, "Daisey Got Me Crazy" in 1962. The film, *The Harder They Come* catapulted Cliff to fame. More successful records followed. Today, he is one of reggae's biggest stars.

What does reggae mean to you?

Reggae is contemporary because it uses so many different forms. It fits the time.

Have you lost contact with your roots as some of your critics insist?

I have always had a universal mind. Always searching. I try out a lot of things, not only musically but philosophically too. I have heard this said about me. Accusations. Everybody is free to say what they want. Critics. The people are not saying that, just the critics. The people say Jimmy is doing what he feels like doing. The people in Jamaica say this.

Is the record industry there still corrupt?

It is not as bad as the old days when there was only one station there. Everybody wants to record music. The owners were tricky. It is hard to get a good break but you have to push on. With determination, you can make it.

■ ■ ■ ■ ■ ■ ■ ■

Toots Hibbert: Reggae's High Priest

In Jamaica, the popularity of Toots Hibbert and the Maytals was surpassed, even by the Wailers. Their fans adore them. Their albums, *Funky Kingston* and *Reggae Got Soul* were huge immediate bestsellers internationally. Here are some excerpts from an interview with Toots:

What is the Devil's music?

Satan is man. Man does bad deeds. God is among the poor. Music of the flesh, no. We worship God. Some people who call themselves Rastafari worship Haile Selassie. But he is a man. I worship God, who made Haile Selassie. People say they are holy but they kill their brother or go in the dark and do evil things.

Satan?

Satan is vanity. Some music is like Satan. Satan does not last, it withers. It is forgotten quickly.

Mot songs, pop songs, are about secular love, love of the flesh. What about sex?

Songs should be of God, of good love, not of bad things. People have turned from the good; but still they look up, up into the blue sky and say they cannot see God. God is not there; he is here. God does not hide anything from us. He tells us everything. God does not want physical things, but he knows we want them so he provides them for us. The music has to be righteous, not about physical things. Like you hear sing of boy and girl in bed, hugging and kissing. "Yeh, yeh love my babe so much, mon." When I sing, I think of Godly things, not worldly things.

How would you describe reggae?

Reggae is an everyday thing. It is suffering put to music. All over Jamaica: it is from the ghetto, from Trenchtown, from people who want but can't get. We sing the words of our people, our music is from the roots.

Of which of the two Rasta religions are you a member?

When you do God's work, you become God. By doing this, you are doing the will of God. You don't have to have a lot of hair; all you have to have is love. You have to do things the way you think God would do them, and love the world the way you love yourself. Hair does not mean a thing. The heart has to be clean, clean.

How does this relate to your music?

Reggae is religious. You can make it be real religious, make the people move. Everyone does not sing it the same; some are different.

Like Bob Marley, for instance.

We are two different singers. He appreciates me; I appreciate him. We have a love for each other. You can hear it in our work.

When you sing, I feel a tingle in my chest like I used to in the church.

I feel it too. The church is in me, in us. The church is in the band. This joy is reggae. We are all brothers; we all were created by one Father.

■ ■ ■ ■ ■ ■ ■ ■

Bob Marley: A Child of Jah

Bob Marley was reggae's first international superstar, mesmerizing audiences with his electrifying concerts and albums. On his final U.S. tour, he talked about life, spiritual purpose, and his music. He died of cancer in 1981.

What does reggae mean for your brothers in places like Trenchtown and elsewhere?

Reggae means feel good, means hope. It brings the people pride, and expresses what they themselves think about the way they live under oppression.

Do you believe Rastas have any political influence in Jamaica? Have they made Mr. Manley implement any positive changes for the people?

No government ever does anything for Rastas in Jamaica. No one can explain why that is up to now, 'cause Jamaica is full of Rastas.

The press would have us believe that you and Mr. Manley are friends, that he wants to make Rastas part of the political systems there.

The Rastas in Jamaica are more than Mr. Manley. He cannot help Rastas because only Rastas can help Rasta. If there is something else than he can help Rasta – if I need food, if I need cow, if I need horse. They can give us only material things, nothing spiritual. We need Rasta men in control, we need a Rasta government.

You often sing about Africa. Recently, you went there for the first time. How did it feel?

I just wanted to get an I-view. It felt good. I felt strong like a warrior. Africa is the homeland.

One of your themes in your latest album, Survival, is the unity of all people of all color. Do you see that happening in our lifetime?

I see it. Everything is possible. But it is important first to have a Rasta government in Jamaica. Mon, the whole world fight against the Black man. Black people should check out Haile Selassie I. Check him out 'cause then we are dealing with our tradition, our culture. We must ask what is this people Marcus Garvey talk about? Our people

Marcus Garvey talk about. We must remember how it is to be a slave. If we are not slaves, whatever we are, we must get freedom right now. 'Cause right now we're neutral, too neutral. Plenty of our people suffer.

Another popular subject for you is Babylon and the superpowers. Is Babylon within the person or is it these colonialist countries? What is the difference?

Babylon is some guides we have set up, a society that is set. For instance, the ideology that runs capitalists and communists. I don't know if you have that any more, that was the two ruling once. All the things they force upon the people – that's Babylon. Babylon is the anti-Christ organization.

The Beast, as in the Bible?

Yeh mon, in control. If we followed our tradition, we, our people, could never be like that. We would be like King David, King Solomon. Good. Respect ourselves, yeh mon. When we mix with the Beast, we are no longer ourselves. We're like lost sheep. We must check ourselves. We must cling to our roots. Be Rasta, a child of Jah.

Pivotal Reggae Pioneers

The following musicians are pivotal, though often unsung, pioneers in the development of reggae. Some you may know, some have been neglected. However, these artists were crucial to the development of the genres that comprise the tributaries of reggae.

This list is not meant to be a full encyclopedic rendition of the musical accomplishments of all the noted artists. Its intent is simply to provide guideposts, a map as it were, that serve to assist the reader in their journey in discovering true reggae gems.

Aswad

According to pundits, Aswad was arguably Britain's most successful reggae band, but it made only modest gains in the U.S. market. A fixture on the British music scene of 1970s and 1980s, their fans hail their early material as the greatest roots reggae Britain ever produced, while others find their later pop-crossover phase more distinctive and unique, although they accuse the band of selling out. Still, Aswad's flexibility to accommodate changing times is the key of their survival in their decades-long career.

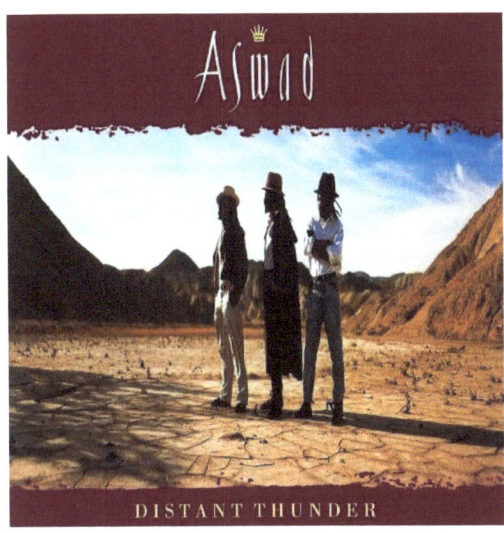
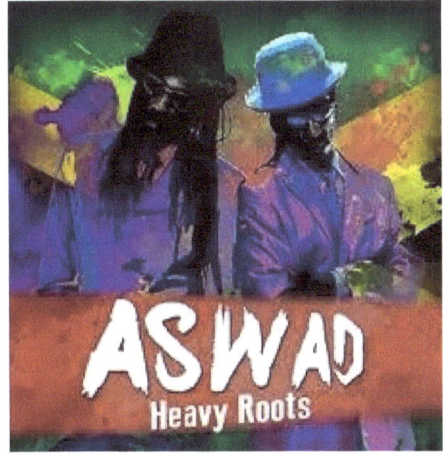

Rasta, Babylon, Jamming

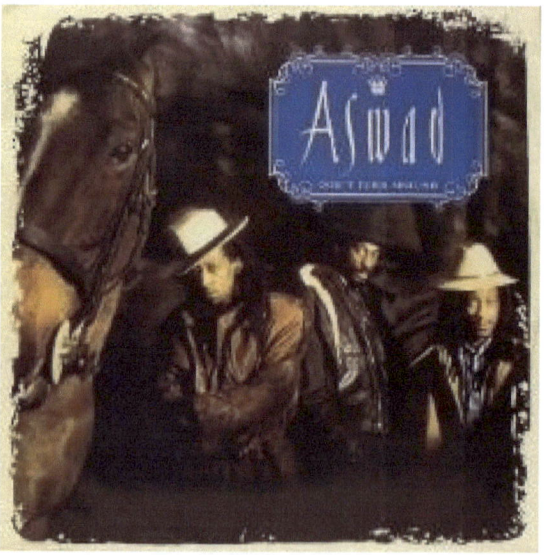

Augustus Pablo

The name of Augustus Pablo, the master mixer of reggae, is revered in Jamaican music. A native of the island, he, aka Horace Swaby, attended Kingston College (not a college in the American sense, but a high school), where he learned the mechanics of the organ. It was here at Kingston College where Pablo made the connections that would help launch him into the music industry. Among his classmates was Clive Chin, whose family ran Randy's, Kingston's premier record store. The Chin clan included Herman Chin Loy, a cousin of Leslie Kong, and who started his own career in the music industry by working for his famous cousin. Loy set up his own record store and label in 1969, both called Aquarius. In 1970, when the 15- year-old Pablo began his own musical career, Aquarius was his first stop. In no time, he was working with producer Lee "Scratch" Perry, mixing material at King Tubby's studio. He was a wizard, using his acclaimed Addis-type sound with his melodica, clavinet, harpsichord, and xylophone. He also used dubs, with echoed horns and guitar stylings. However, Pablo's best known recording, a dub classic, "King Tubby Meets The Rockers Uptown" (1975), which has been remixed many times by various producers throughout the years. His masterwork is the treasured East of the River trilogy (1978). He seized on the concepts of dancehall and made it his own, often packing audiences around the world in the 1980s and 1990s. His music had a sizeable fan base in Japan, where his records sold very well. Unfortunately, Pablo became afflicted with myasthenia gravis, a rare nerve disease in the late 1980s, which killed him in 1999.

Barrington Levy

Following the death of Bob Marley in 1981, Barrington Levy, arrived on the dancehall scene and soon established himself as a performer with staying power. He captured the market and topped the charts well into the '90s. A native of Jamaica, Levy formed the Mighty Multitude with his cousin Everton Dacres. They cut their first single, "My Black Girl," in 1977. At 14, Levy broke out on his own the next year and recorded his debut solo single, "A Long Time Since We Don't Have No Love." It didn't have much of an impact, but the teen's appearances filled the dancehalls and were talked about in

the music industry. At one of these shows, Levy met two producers and the pair took the youth into Channel One studio. With the Roots Radics, they recorded a few sides, including "Ah Yah We Deh," "Looking My Love," "Englishman," and "Wedding Ring Aside." Success was immediate, but it was the hit, "Collie Weed," followed by a series of smash singles in 1978-1980 that really made him popular. He continued his winning streak with "Wicked Intention," "Jumpy Girl," a lovely version of Horace Andy's "Skylarking," "Reggae Music," and "Wicked Intention." He knocked them dead at in shows at Reggae Sunsplash in 1980 and 1981. The singer joined forces with producer Alvin Ranglin for another sting of hits -- "Never Tear My Love Apart," "Jah," "You Made Me So Happy," and "When You're Young and in Love." The hit, "Revelation, produced by Lloyd Dennis, got him a tour to England, where he earned a Best Vocalist award at the UK Reggae Award show.

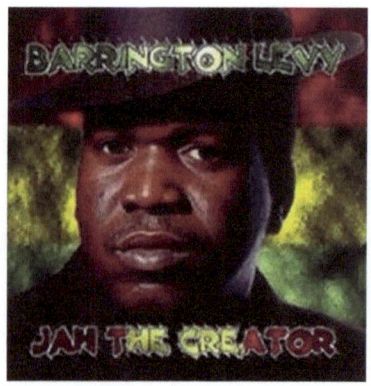

Big Youth

An early advocate of Rasta culture, Big Youth, aka Manley Buchanan, was one of the premier DJs, the consummate cultural toaster, ruling the dancehalls in the '70s. Some say he was the first to wear dreadlocks on stage in the 1973. His career stalled in the next decade as other musical styles emerged, but he burst back on top in the '90s. . Born

in Kingston, Jamaica, Buchanan had his moniker of Big Youth long before he had picked up a mic. He was named by his co-workers at the Kingston Sheraton hotel, where the tall teen was employed as a mechanic. He recorded his debut, "Screaming Target" in 1973, with a faithful following. Initially, he toasted with some creative, free vocals, inspired by the modern jazz giants such as Charlie Parker, Dizzy, and Coltrane, along with the phrasing of female soul singers. His mother was a preacher, so he got his spiritual bent naturally.

When he saw the restraints placed on performers by record companies, he started his own labels, and profited solidly. He scored with the big hit, "Hit The

Road Jack" from his double album, "Reggae Phenomenon" in 1974. Two other albums, "Natty Universal Dread" (1976) and "Isaiah First Prophet of Old (1978), which he believes is his

best recording to date. His album, "Higher Grounds" (1995) allowed his fans to know he could still rock the house. His performances are still memorable at Reggae Sunsplash in 1983, 1987, 1992, and 1996.

Black Uhuru

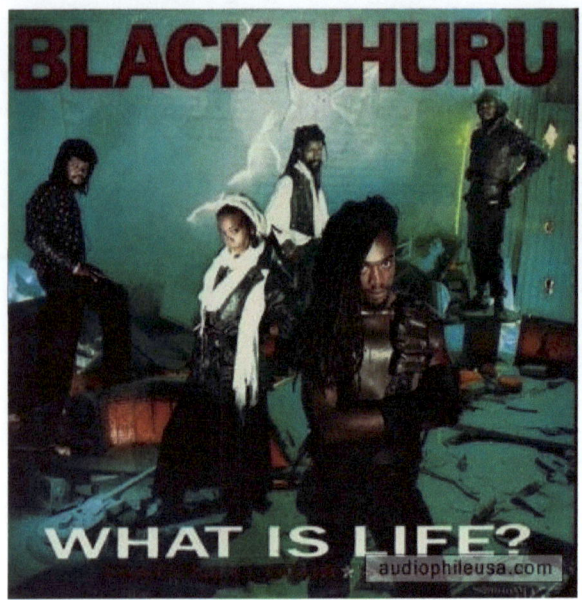

One of the most revered of the second-generation reggae bands, Black Uhuru maintained their sizeable audience globally despite many personnel changes in their 40-plus-year history. As the first reggae band to win a Grammy award for their 1983 album, "Anthem," Black Uhuru was reputed to be one of the most exciting reggae acts of the music's Golden Age. The band, whose name comes from the Swahili word meaning "freedom," was formed in Kingston by Don Carlos, Rudolph "Garth" Dennis, and Derrick "Duckie" Simpson. When the group experienced difficulties securing a record contract, it shuffled its lineup and Simpson reorganized the band with Errol "Jay" Wilson and lead vocalist Michael Rose. Joined by the classic rhythm section of Sly Dunbar on drums and Robbie Shakespeare on bass, Black Uhuru created a sound that made them second to none. Their debut album, Love Crisis, released in 1977, included the anthem, "I Love King Selassie." They found gold with other hits, "General Penitentiary, Guess Who's Coming To Dinner (1978) and "Plastic Smile and Shine Eye Gal (1979). Wilson was replaced by Sandra "Puma" Jones, an American dancer. The group's popularity was assured by a group of smash albums: "Sensemilla" (1981), "Red" (1981), "Tear It Up" (1982) and "Chill Out" (1982). Critically praised, "Red" was cited as one of the top 100 albums of the 1980s and "Tear It Up" was recognized as one of the best live albums in reggae. Group squabbles and issues with Island Records brought hard times, which Simpson said the company tricked them with a bad contract. However, the "Anthem" Grammy triumph in 1983 was offset by further losses,

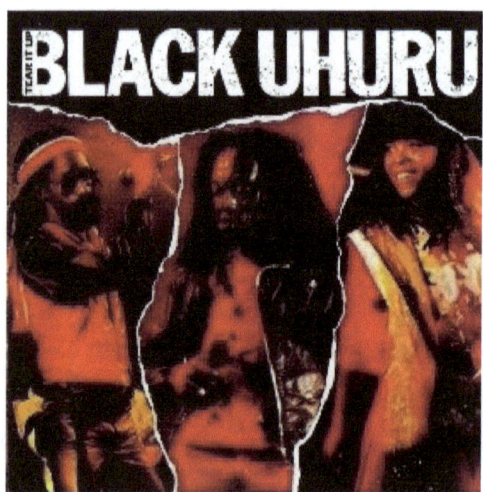

including the death of Puma by cancer in 1990. The 1990s also saw experimenting with the hip-hop sound on their album, "Now" and some dancehall flavor on "Unification" in 1998. In 2001, "Dynasty was released, and the band sputtered into inaction.

Bunny Wailer

As a founding member of the Wailers, and the trio's only surviving member, Bunny Wailer, has become a respected elder statesmen of the Jamaican music scene. His vocal and composing contributions to the Wailers had continued the legacy of that pioneering group. Born Neville O' Riley Livingston in 1947 in Kingston, he spent his earliest years in St. Ann's, where he first met Bob Marley. They became fast friends. Singer Joe Higgs, who rose to stardom in the late '50s, helped other young talent around the

neighborhood, and gave singing lessons in his tenement yard on Third Street. Higgs nurtured their talent, along with another gifted pair, Peter Tosh and Junior Braithwaite. After a failed audition for producer Leslie Kong, the four boys joined forces, along with backing singers Cherry Green and Beverly Kelso, to become the Teenagers. The band's name would change several times before they finally settled on the Wailing Wailers. Bunny's songwriting talents quieted over time, but he produced some hits: "What Am I Supposed To Do?", "Tread Oh," along with "Riding High" and Dreamland" with Lee "Scratch Perry. He felt overshadowed by Marley but it was conflicts during the UK tour that posed a problem for him. As a strict Rastafarian, he couldn't eat processed food so he often went hungry during the tour. He remained as a Wailer until 1973, and made just two shows for the group - two benefit shows in 1974 and 1975.

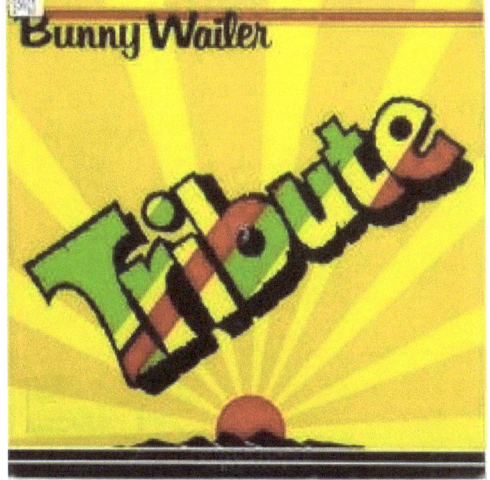

He debuted his album, "Blackheart Man" (1976) and

other music in three years later, "Bright Soul," "Free Jah Children" and "Rise and Shine." He hated touring. However, he returned to the stage in 1982. In 1987, he released two more albums, "Rude Man Skanking" and "Rude Dance Hall." He got a Grammy for "Crucial! Roots Classics" (1995) and two Grammys for his Marley tributes, "Time Will Tell" (1990), "Hall of Fame (1995).

Burning Spear

One of the most brilliant and respected roots artists in Jamaica's music history, Burning Spear (aka Winston Rodney) has advocated the tenets of black history and culture into the island's mainstream society. Taking his name from a symbol popularized by Kenyan Mau Mau freedom fighter Jomo Kenyatta, he remains faithful to his core themes of oppression of black race, the teachings of Marcus Garvey, and repatriation to Africa, the Motherland. The group, Burning Spear, is second only in acclaim to Bob Marley and the Wailers internationally. Born in St. Ann's Bay, Jamaica in 1948, Rodney befriended Marley, who recommended the singer  venture to Studio One chief Coxsone Dodd. Rodney recorded a debut single, "Door Peep" (1969). Teamed with bandmates Rupert Wellington and Delroy Hines, they released their debut album, "Marcus Garvey" in 1975 with high praise from the critics. Taking a break, Rodney did a series of singles: "Free Black People, Spear Burning," and "Traveling." The band hit its stride with three albums, "Burning Spear Live" (1977), "Social Living" (1978), and its last major release before urban unrest struck the island, "Hail HIM" (1980).

While Jamaica erupted, Rodney moved to Queens, N.Y., seeking some serenity to put his life back together. However, the band was never far from his mind. Burning Spear returned with a vengeance, recording several successful albums: "Resistance" (1985), "People of the World" (1986) and "Rasta Business" (1995). At their peak, the band took home two Grammys for Best Reggae Record with "Calling Rastafari" (1999) and "Jah Is Real" (2009).

Ijahman Levi

One of the spiritual ambassadors of the Rastafari movement, Ijahman Levi, aka Trevor Sutherland, a native of Jamaica, learned his craft from accomplished musician and vocal teacher, Joe Higgs. When he moved to England, he was sentenced to a three-year term in prison for domestic violence with his first wife. He took the name, Ijahman Levi after a religious conversion to the Rastafari movement when he was in prison between 1972 and 1974. His debut single release, "Jah Heavy Load" and the following records such as "Haile I Know" (1978) and "Are We A Warrior" (1979) preach the themes of the Rastafari movement as well as the spiritual concept of the Twelve Tribes of Israel doctrine. When a legal battle between Levi and Island occurred, the singer moved to control his publishing rights. With the 1982 release, "Tell It To the Children," reached the store, Levi knew he possessed full authority over his music, recording, packaging, and marketing. In 1985, he released "I Do," a duet with his second wife, Madge. The song did well on the British reggae charts, reaching near the top. To date, he has released over forty albums of his signature sound.

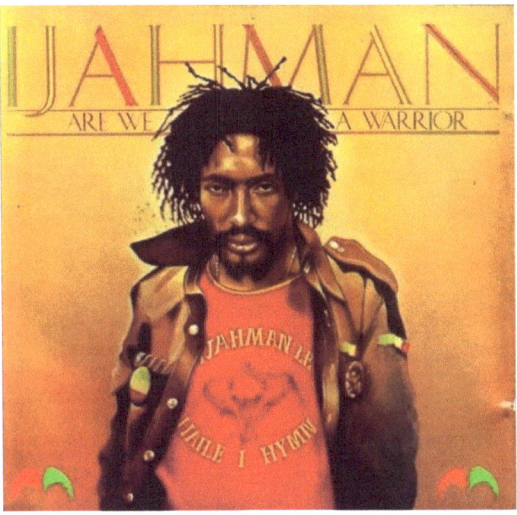

Jimmy Cliff

In a long career that has spanned from singing ska in the 1960s to the present on the Jamaican music scene, Jimmy Cliff has survived the ever changing trends in popular taste. Some say Cliff has failed to reach potential, while others have recognized the versatility and durability of the artist. Born in St. James, Jamaica as James Chambers, his singing talent was apparent in his early years as he started his career singing at local shows and parish fairs. At age 14, he moved to Kingston, took the last name of Cliff, and recorded two lackluster singles before he was approached by singer Derrick Morgan and recommended to ace producer Leslie Kong. His first single, "Hurricane Hattie" was an instant success. His loyalty to Kong remained to the man's untimely death. However, by a string of follow-up hits, Cliff and Kong set new standards on the ska scene in those early years, both in Jamaica and in Britain. Music historians consider those fledgling works, "Miss Jamaica," "King of Kings," "One Eyed Jacks," and "Pride and Passion" as classics of the original ska era.

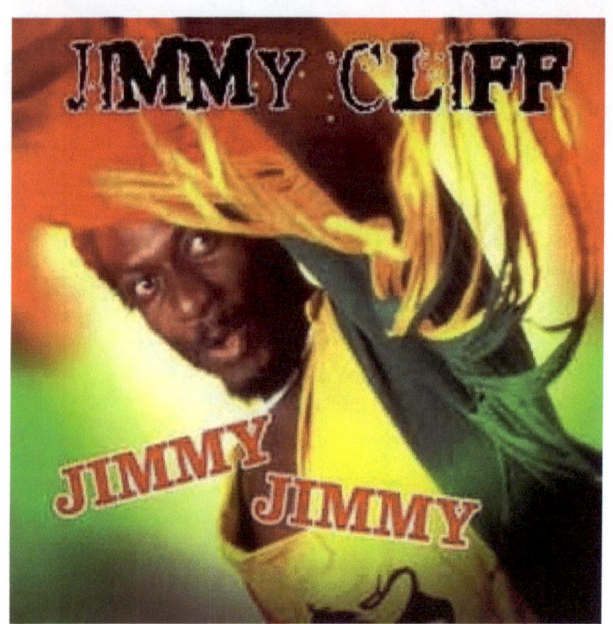

By 1964, Cliff was selected as one of Jamaica's musical representatives at the World's Fair. A successful residency in Paris followed, and Island head Chris Blackwell eventually convinced the singer to relocate to Britain. In 1969, he released "Hard Road To Travel" under the Island label. Then the singer reversed his fortunes with his big hit, "Wonderful World, Beautiful People" (1969) and an anti-war hymn, "Vietnam," which Bob Dylan said it was one of the best protest songs he'd ever heard. Cliff followed up with another smash single, "You Can Get It If You Really Want" (1970) and that rush of good luck was interrupted by the loss of Kong. Being the musical chameleon that he was, Cliff recorded a 1971 experiment, "Another Cycle," which featured no reggae but stressed R&B elements. It was recorded in the U.S. using the famed Muscle Shoals studio. Ever striving, Cliff portrayed the role, Rhygin, a folk hero of the Jamaican poor, in the highly commercial film, "The Harder They Come." The role widened his international status. In 1973, the singer released "Unlimited," a blend of reggae-pop fare, and went into Islam during a visit to Africa, but moved away from the religion in 1977. During this period, he also recorded two other works, "Struggling Man" and "House of Exile." A tour to the U.S. in the 1980s led Cliff's foray with several American labels, MCA, Warner Brothers, and Columbia Records, with average product like "I Am The Living," "Give The People What They Want," "Special," and The Power and the Glory." In 1985, Cliff earned the second reggae Grammy ever awarded and followed up with "Hanging Fire" (1988), recorded partly in Congo. He tried other sound mixes in his music, including a collaboration with Tim Armstrong in a punk-rock band, Rancid. Ultimately, Cliff has been always challenging the boundaries of Jamaican music.

Asked about roots reggae, Cliff told a reporter: "Roots...roots and culture...call it whatever you like...was a necessity at the time. The times called for some sort of positive stance by black people in Jamaica because of the way things turned out after independence."

Joe Gibbs

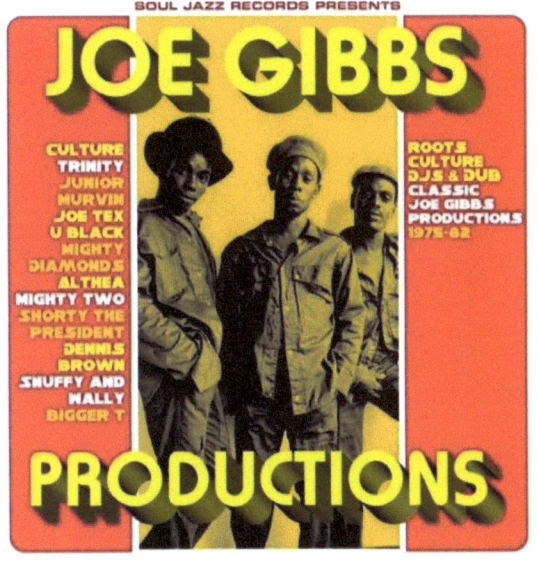

Premier producer Joe Gibbs, aka Joel A. Gibson, learned the music business from the ground up. At the beginning, he sold records in his TV repair shop in Kingston. Without the benefit of the customary sound system, Gibbs funded recording sessions with Lee "Scratch" Perry, the excellent producer of Amalgamated Records. From the early days of rocksteady to '80s dancehall, Gibbs put together a slew of hits by such island stars as the Pioneers, Dennis Brown, the Heptones, Culture, Frankie Paul, and Nicky Thomas. Along with his contemporary, producer Bunny "Striker" Lee, Gibbs is legendary in finding talents among the most important of Jamaica's musical giants, not just over the many years of his illustrious career, but with the satisfying series of quality hits.

Further exploring the local music scene, Gibbs soon began to strike out with independent projects, with installing a two-track studio in the back of his shop. Along with the already established Perry, he recruited the gifted Winston "Niney" Holness, then Errol Thompson to act as studio engineer for his label after Niney's exit. During this entire time, Gibbs' Amalgamated label kept creating successes, including his first single, Roy Shirley's "Hold Them," that would eventually be called the first rocksteady song.

In the late 1970s, Amalgamated was extremely profitable with the dynamic duo of Thompson and Perry, notably with several popular vocal groups and instrumentals. Some of the label's stars featured on the label: Delroy Wilson, Nicky Thomas, Judy Mowatt, the Immortals, the Slickers, the Young Souls, Junior Byles, Peter Tosh, and Dennis Brown. There was some backlash against Gibbs when some musicians accused him of cheating them out of royalties. Even Perry turned against him, recording the scathing "People Funny Boy." Harassed by debtors, Gibbs was put out of business in 1980 after a legal battle over copyrights. In 2008, he died of a heart attack.

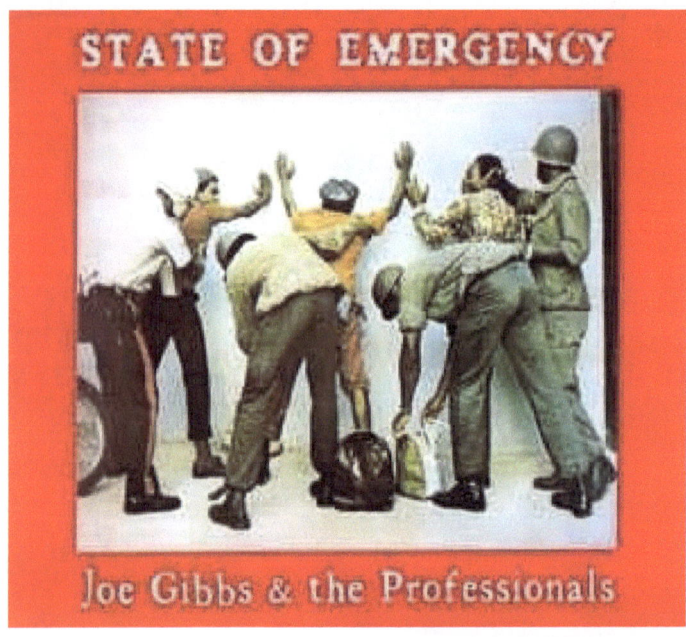
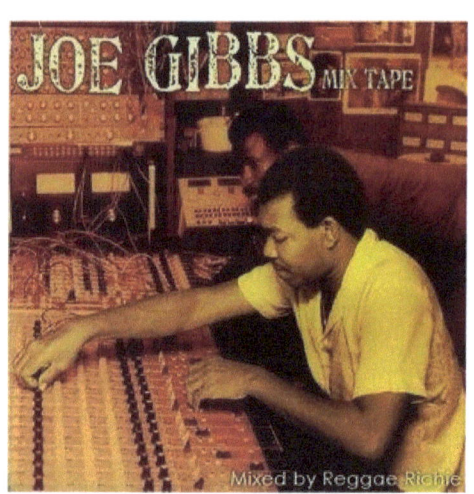

Judy Mowatt

One-third of the I-Threes, reggae's most influential female vocal trio, Judy Mowatt was one of the music's popular female artists. Born in Kingston, she joined as a lead singer of the R&B female trio, the Gaylettes in 1967. They performed a blend of R&B and Jamaican dance music, playing tribute to the Motown girl groups such as The Supremes and The Marvelettes. The group split in 1970. Mowatt's breakthrough occurred when she was hired by vocalist Marcia Griffiths along with Rita Marley, the wife of Bob, to sing background on a track in 1974. The trio of Mowatt, Marley and Griffiths later became the I-Threes, and a part of Bob Marley's performance entourage. Mowatt's first album, "Mellow Mood," appeared on Marley's Tuff Gong label, and later she became a member of the Rastafarian movement. It was only fate that she was not there to witness the Marley's assassination attempt in 1976 at his compound, where several people were injured. Her output was sparse but powerful: "Black Woman" (1979), "Only a Woman" (1982), "Working Wonders" (1985), "Look at Love" (1991), "Sing Our Own Song" (2002), and Something Old, Something New" (2002). She converted to Christianity in 1995. Calling herself a reggae gospel singer, she does charity work for women prisoners and the poor.

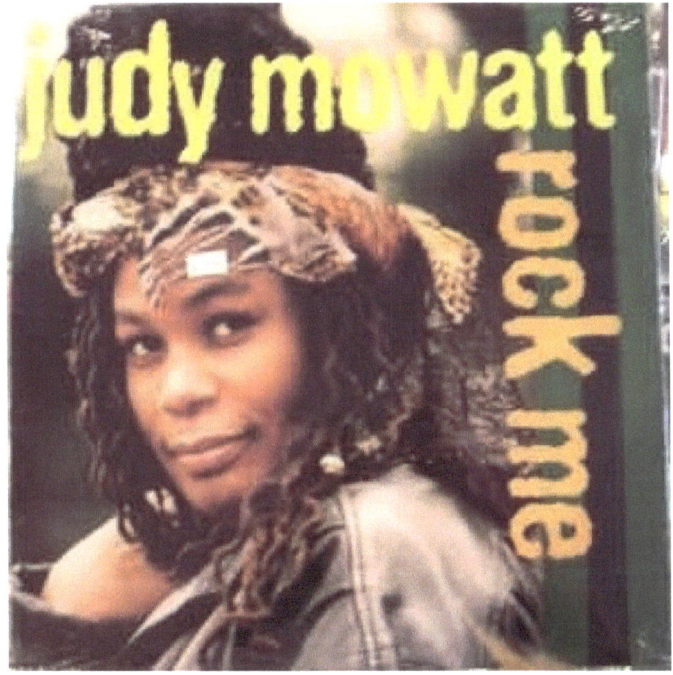

Peter Tosh

Singer, musician, composer, and rebel Peter Tosh promised his people that he would make his mark on the Jamaican musical scene. He did just that, both as a founding member of the Wailers and as a solo artist. He toured with the Rolling Stones and had an international hit with a duet with Mick Jagger, then toured again before adoring crowds around the world as the headlining act.

Born Winston Hubert McIntosh in the small rural village of Grange Hill, Jamaica, he spent some childhood years with an aunt, then moved with an uncle in Trenchtown at age 15. In Kingston, he found his way to Joe Higgs' tenement yard, joining other aspiring youths eager for his vocal coaching lessons. Among the local teens were Bunny Wailer, Bob Marley, and Junior Braithwaite. The trio of Tosh, Marley, and Wailer became the Wailing Wailers, modeling themselves after the American soul groups.

In 1969, Lee Perry recorded the young group and later sold the session master tapes to an English label, Trojan. They were outraged when the label released the albums, "Soul Rebels" (1970), "Soul Revolution" (1971, and "African Herbsman" (1973). However, the fortunes of the Wailers changed with the arrival of Island Records boss, Chris Blackwell and the new album, "Catch A Fire" (1973), that brought them much media attention. That year, Tosh co-wrote the resistance song, "Get Up, Stand Up" with Marley. A scant six months later, another album, "Burnin'" was released and it was the final date of Tosh appeared as a member. Tosh felt Blackwell was only interested in Marley as a headliner and not the rest of the trio.

Tosh was not idle. He recorded "Legalize It," a pro-weed anthem, in 1976, which scored big in the U.K and was an underground smash in the U.S. He followed it up the next year with "Equal Rights," which detailed many of his more personal militant themes. Tosh toured in 1978 with his band, Word, Sound & Power, which consisted of Sly & Robbie, and many of Marley's old group. Politically outspoken, Tosh called for the destruction of both leaders, Michael Manley and Edward Seaga, which made him a marked man. As the singer said to reporters, his words irritated the politicians:
"They know that I speak the truth, and the truth is destructive to the functioning of lies and corruption." Later, he signed a contract with the Rolling Stones Records. His album for the label, "Bush Doctor" (1978), featured a duet with Tosh and Jagger. The later albums continued his political and cultural concepts: "Mystic Man" (1979), "Wanted Dread & Alive" (1981) and "No Nuclear War" (1987). Still bold and controversial, Tosh was assassinated in 1987 in a home invasion by three gunmen.

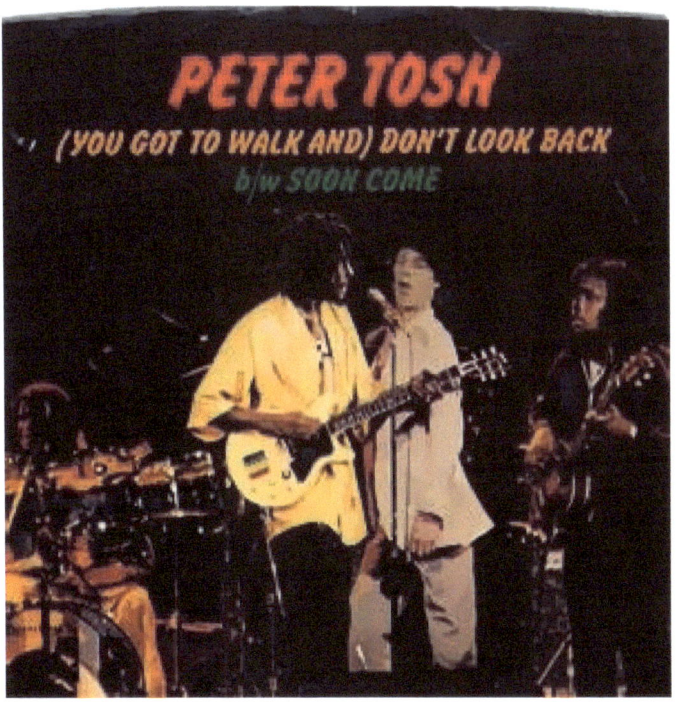

Ras Michael

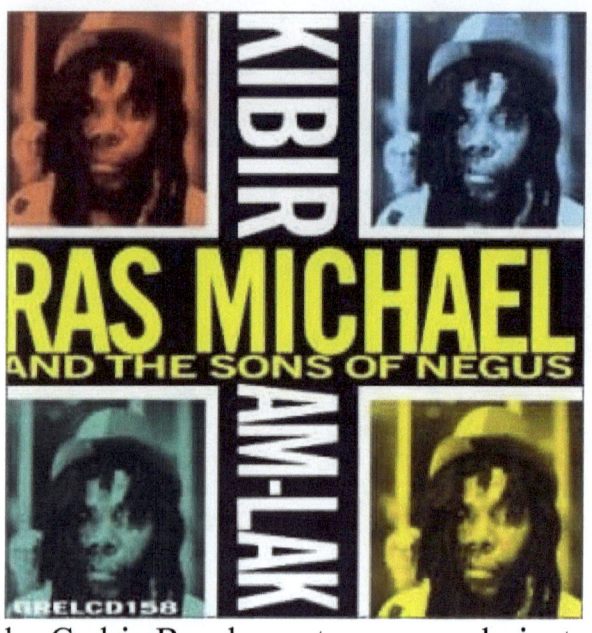

No musical group honored the Rasta principles like Ras Michael and The Sons of Negus. In fact, Negus paid homage to the memory of Ethiopian Emperor Haile Selassie I, the Almighty God of the Rastafarian movement. This was pure Rasta music. Ras Michael and his group, the Sons of Negus, performed elements of Nyahbingi music, which was played in Rastafarian meetings and ceremonies. Born Michael George Henry, he, a drummer, led Rasta groups since the mid-1960s, with an aggregation of percussionists, horn men, guitarists, and chanters. This group was led by Cedric Brooks on tenor sex, clarinet and flute. Their praise is the beat of the heart, based on the original "instrument of ten strings," and the hand-beaten drum. The group was also deeply influenced by the teachings of Marcus Garvey. On 1975's "Dadawah," Michael took a religious ceremony as the theme for an album of lyrical poetry with raw, visceral power. Other albums followed: "Rastafari" (1975), "Kibir-Am-Lak" (1978), "Movements" (1978), "Love Thy Neighbour" (1979), "Revelation" (1982), "Zion Train" (1988), and "Medicine Man" (2007).

Later, abandoning minimalism, the group's current works added electronics, funk, rock, and blues.

Sister Carol

One of the dancehall era's few powerful female DJs, Sister Carol was reggae's strong, positive feminist voice who was inspired by her Rastafarian faith and never catered to sexual enticements to seduce an audience. Born Carol Theresa East in Kingston, she took the stage name of Sister Carol, although she had previously used others, including Black Cinderella and Mother Culture. At age 14, she moved with her family to Brooklyn N.Y., where her father was an engineer with Radio Jamaica and involved in recording sessions at Studio One. She earned a degree in education from the City College of New York in 1981 and gave birth to her first child.  Her first big break came when she was advised by Brigadier Jerry, a Jamaican DJ, to do DJ chatting in dancehall style. Her debut album, "Liberation for Africa" was released as a limited edition on the Jamaican SG label in 1983. That next year, "Black Cinderella" was marketed to the stores. She formed her own label. Other albums include: "Jah Disciple" (1989), "Call Mi Sister Carol" (1994), "Potent Dub" (1997) "Isis- The Original Rasta Womb-man" (1999), "IDerful Words" (2006), "Togetherness" (2012) and "Live No Evil" (2014).

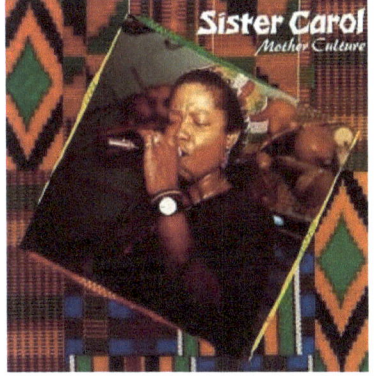

She was one of only three women in the reggae world to be nominated for a Grammy – Judy Mowatt (1986), Rita Marley (1992) and Sister Carol (1997). She was more of a singjay than a full-time toaster, capable of surprising vocals as well as catchy rhymes. As an actress, she appeared in several Jonathan Demme films, such as "Something Wild" (1986), "Married To The Mob" (1988) and Rachel Getting Married" (2008). Never quite a dominant force in the marketplace, she worked regularly and enjoyed critical acclaim. In the 2000s, she returned to Jamaica.

Sly & Robbie

The collaboration of these two supreme musical talents, drummer Sly Dunbar and bassist Robbie Shakespeare has been the driving rhythmic force behind countless songs -- one statistic noted the duo played on approximately 200,000 tracks, and that total doesn't count the additional remixes, versions, and dubs. As a production team, they were the pioneering avant-garde edge of modern dub, ragga, and dancehall.

Dunbar and Shakespeare, known as the Rhythm Twins, joined forces in 1975. Both musicians grew up in Kingston, loyal fans of American country-and-western songs. They first worked as a studio sidemen for Channel One, lending their skills to a group, The Revolutionaries. During the second half of the 1970s, they became an important team on the Jamaican scene, both in the studio and on tour. Their musicianship provided for so many established stars such as Ijahman Levi, Culture, Peter Tosh, Gregory Issacs, Black Uhuru, Bob Dylan, Grace Jones, Ali Campbell, Maxi Priest, Simply Red, and Keith Richards, among others. Other albums include: "Sly Dunbar: Simple Sly Man" (1978), "Sly Wicked & Slick" (1979), "Sly & Robbie: Raiders of the Lost Dub" (1981), "Language Barrier" (1995), "Riddim: Best of Sly & Robbie in Dub 1978-1985" (2004) and "Blackwood Dub" (2012). The pair continue to be active as session men and tour occasionally with their own band.

Sugar Minott

Fans of Jamaica's exciting dancehall scene all knew Sugar Minott as a thrilling performer who never failed to satisfy his audience. His music provided the musical template for the ingredients of the contemporary dancehall style. A multi-threat, he was also very capable as a producer, and his highly popular sound system launched many new DJs into the limelight.

Born Lincoln Barrington Minott in Kingston, he began his career in the sound systems as a youngster, working as a selector for the Sound of Silence Keystone outfit. Later, he started his own Gathering of Youth sound system, using skills gained from his previous job. In 1969, Minott decided to take the mike as a singer, becoming one third of the African Brothers roots trio, working their way around the amateur talent show circuit. On the Micron label, African Brothers, with Minott, released a number of singles over the next few years, including "Party Night," "Mysterious Nature," Lead Us Father," "Gimme Gimme African Love," "Youth of Today," and "A Di System" cut with producer Jah Bunny. The trio split in 1974. Minott went solo, landing among the stars at Studio One. His 1978 debut album, "Live Loving," was considered the first dancehall album. The next record, "Black Roots," was released in 1979 and made it possible for him to move to England. He became a notable reggae name in the UK with "Ghetto-Ology Plus Dub" (1979,) which was reissued with additional dubs by the Jamaican wizard King Tubby. A few subsequent albums solidified Minott's reputation such as "Sugar Minott at Studio One (2004), "New Day" (2008), and "Reggae Legends" (2010). The singer cancelled his Canadian tour that year due to chest pains. Later, he died of heart problems at age 54 in 2010.

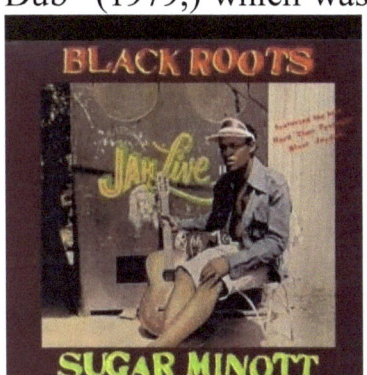

The Mighty Diamonds

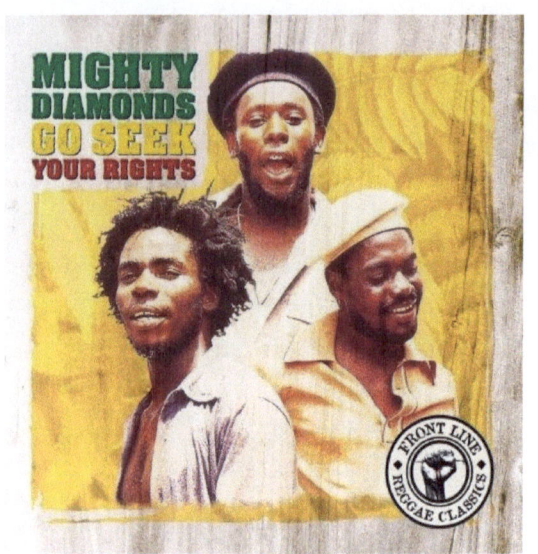

As one of the most internationally popular reggae groups in the '70s roots era, the Mighty Diamonds formed in late 1969 in Kingston, attracting fans with their tight soulful vocal harmonies and imaginative songwriting. In their early years, they tried several producers, creating singles for Lee Perry, Rupie Edwards, Bunny Lee and Jah Lloyd. Channel One studio was the perfect fit for the group, who were devout Rastafarians. The Chinese-Jamaican brothers Hoo-Kim brothers worked out a marketable formula that blended their spiritual and political themes with romantic material, which gave them a more commercial appeal than other groups. However, the group later signed with Virgin Records as the label sought to expand their share in the reggae market. Their debut record, "Right Time" (1976), immediately captured public attention.

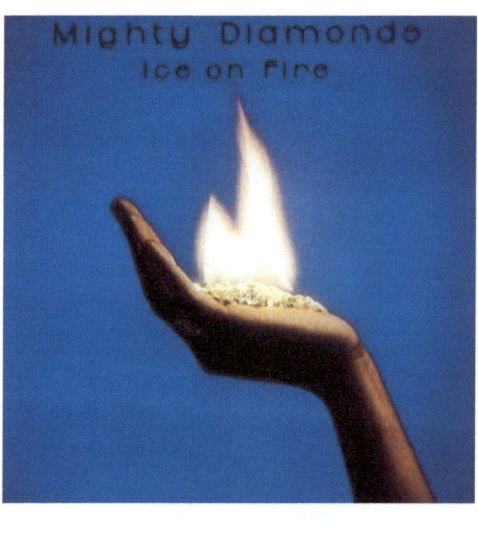

The line-up of Mighty Diamonds, from its beginning, consisted of founder and harmony singer Pat "Lloyd" Ferguson (aka Judge Diamond, the Judge), lead singer Donald Shaw (aka Tabby Diamond or the Prophet), and harmony singer Fitzroy Simpson (aka Bunny Diamond, the Jester).

In 1977 and 1978, they showcased their sound on such as hit-and-miss dates as "Ice on Fire," "Planet Earth," and Stand Up for Judgment." But they scored as a supporting act at the anti-violence One Love Peace Concert in Jamaica in 1978. As the island endured political mayhem in 1979, they tried to capture their follower's interest by returning them to their richness of their culture and traditions, recording two sides: "Deeper Roots" and "Deeper Dub." Legal woes plagued the group for a time until Gussie Clarke's Music Work's label released two records, "The Real Enemy" (1987) and "Get Ready" (1988), with an uncustomary dancehall flair. With a loyal crowd, the band still tours constantly.

The Upsetters

Producer Lee "Scratch" Perry's longtime house band, the Upsetters, were featured on some of the most historic records in reggae, including the early hits of the Wailers. The group was named after Perry's 1968 smash hit, "The Upsetter," with the Upsetter tag  also applied to his record label. Perry was known to switch material and line-ups, according to whoever was in the studio when recording began. Included in the Upsetters' ranks were such talented Jamaican musicians as the versatile brothers Aston and Carlton Barrett, Sly Dunbar, Glen Adams, Winston Wright and Boris Gardiner. Scoring a handful of their own hits, including 1969's "Return of Django" " Rhythm Shower" (1973) and "Blackboard Jungle Dub" (1973), the unit was best known as a support act, enjoying their greatest influence through the records they made during the late 1960s and early 1970s with the Wailers, including the seminal "Duppy Conqueror," "Small Axe" and "Soul Rebel." The band also recorded for produces Sonia Pottinger, Bunny Lee and Lloyd Daley. After 1973, Perry established the infamous Black Ark studio, and found global acceptance with 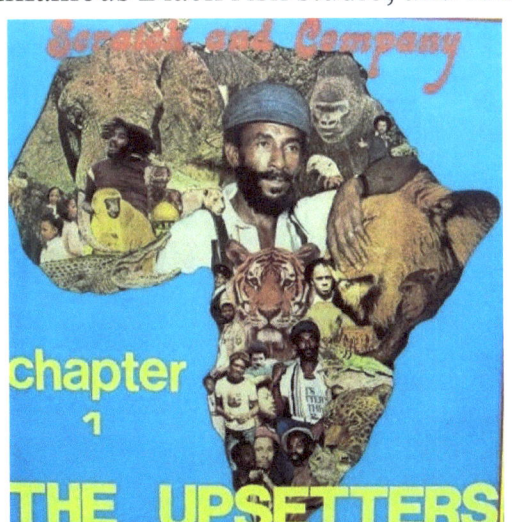 many artists by licensing with Island Records. He had been vital to every artist and the product's production, recording, pressing, distribution, and sales. Singers and  bands came to Black Ark to sample Perry's creativity at adapting their music to his particular sonic frontiers with dub experiments. Unfortunately, there were some doubt of Perry's psychological state. It was confirmed when Black Ark was gutted by a fire, supposedly set by Perry. In 1984, he moved off the island, having residences between London and New York, and eventually settling down in Switzerland in 1989.

Toots & The Maytals

Although they never achieved the commercial impact of Bob Marley and The Wailers, the fan base of Toots & the Maytals believe the band is second to none in the history of Jamaican music. Like many groups, the Maytals prospered through retooling their presentation and content as ska gave way to rocksteady and then evolved into reggae. The group featured lead singer Frederick "Toots" Hibbert, one of the island's most soulful singers and charismatic talents. Between 1961-1962, Toots joined with two Maytals singers, Jerry Mathias and Raleigh Gordon and shortly they were recording tracks at Dodd's Studio One. Toots said they made no money. In 1964, they made "Broadway Jungle" for producer Prince Buster, with the accomplished Skatalites as their backup band. In 1966, Toots was busted for marijuana possession and sentenced to prison, curtailing the Maytals' rise to fame. When the singer was released in 1967, he penned a song, "54-46," a prideful tune about his jail time. Kong produced the song and it became a solid success. The newly reformed group, Maytals, redefined their links between Jamaican sounds and American R&B. Their lead singer's rich, emotive vocal style was informed by Otis Redding, Wilson Pickett, and other soul icons. Some say the group's 1968 release, "Do The Reggay," which was the first song to use the term, reggae.

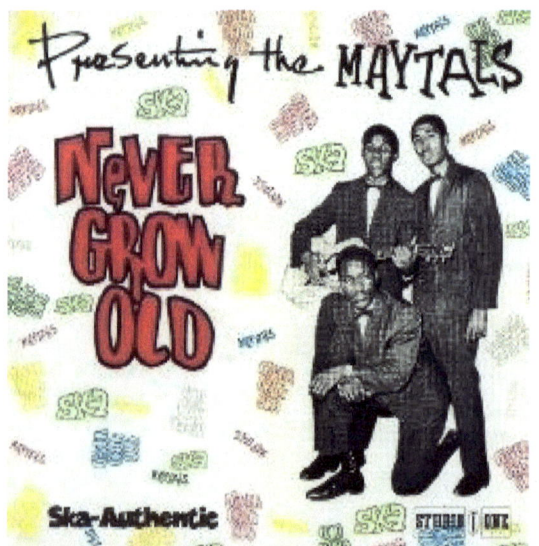

With the untimely death of Kong, their mentor, the Maytals signed with the Dynamic Sounds label, earning the interest of Island Records. Island focused on the 1972 soundtrack of the film, "The Harder They Come," and marketed the Maytals' song, "Pressure Drop" to become a reggae classic. In 1975, Maytals' album, "Funky Kingston" was released in America and well received. While the band continued to tour, it released three more records: "Reggae Got Soul" (1976), "Toots in Memphis" (1988). The Memphis album earned a Grammy nomination. However, the group disbanded in the early 1980s, Toots Hibbert went solo, but an 2004 album, "True Love," a collection of Maytals classics sung by famous singers, won a Grammy award that next year. Putting together a new group, Toots and the Maytals cut tracks for the 2010 "Flip and Twist" record, maintaining a redesigned tour schedule.

Yellowman

Jamaica's first dancehall superstar, Yellowman, born Winston Foster, filled the void in reggae music following Bob Marley's death. His early-'80s success, built on a series of raw singles, raised the popularity of toasting -- the reggae equivalent of rapping – into the mainstream and established dancehall as the new musical wave of the future. Some critics have said Yellowman has demeaned the fine traditions of Jamaican music. They blast his performance style with its "coarse and vulgar" songs and dancehall's penchant for "slack" lyrics -- that is, casual violence, sexism, homophobia, and general rudeness. Graphic sexuality was his particular hook for his listeners, reaching levels of explicitness previously unheard in Jamaica. This controversy was also a big reason for his early popularity. His supporters believe Yellowman's boldness and candor is what makes him special.

What hard challenges has Yellowman weathered in his life! He was an early, constant target for insults and bullying due to his albinism. The shy child grew up in a Catholic institution in Kingston, with only music to quiet his boredom. Inspired by early toasting DJs like U-Roy, he practiced rhyming and got a job with the Gemini Sound System as a substitute DJ. Marketing himself as Yellowman and dressing in a bright yellow suit, the performer peppered his lyrics with jokes about his skin color and lewd tales of his sexual conquests. In 1979, he won a landslide victory at the well-known Tastee Talent Contest, where DJs battled for supremacy. Yellowman overcame all odds to become one of Jamaica's top concert draws after signing as the first dancehall artist to be signed in 1981 to a major American label, Columbia Records.

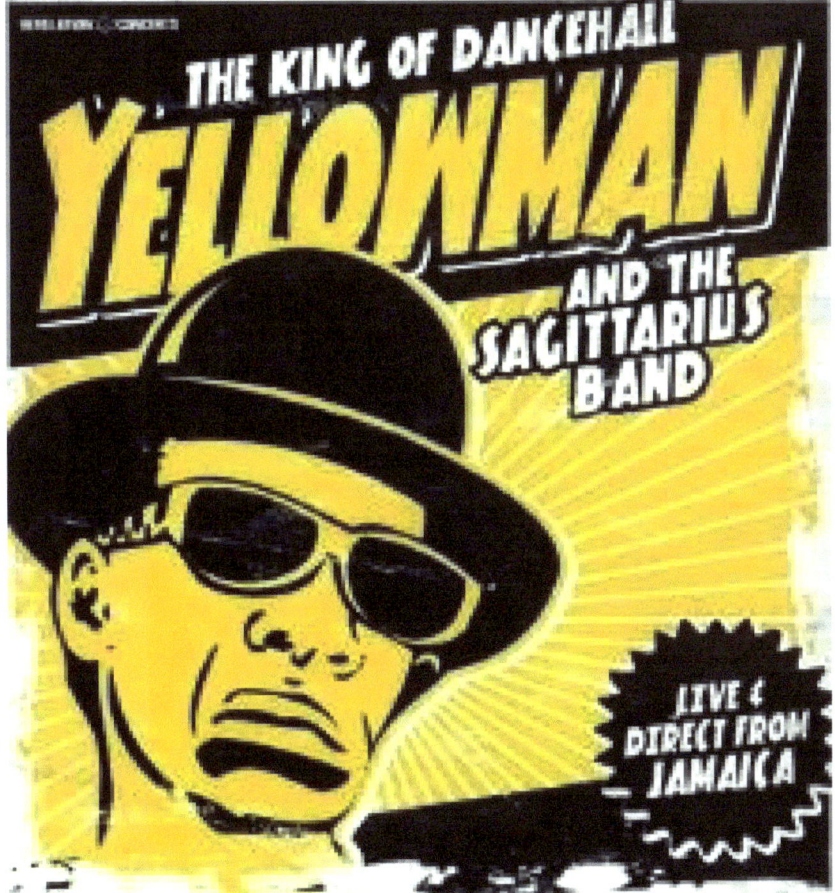

Indeed, Yellowman was recognized as one of the most verbally glib toasters of his time, featuring a free form, relaxed flow with image and substance, a talent for spontaneity, and a quick satirical quality in his wordplay. Fans were dazzled with all his boasting about his skill on the mic and between the sheets. He realized he had to be outlandish, shocking, and slightly vulgar to fill the seats at shows. His first album, "Mister Yellowman" (1982), along with "Zungguzungguguzunguzeng," brought him praise among America's hip-hop royalty and drew countless listeners to his shows. He was the absolute ruler of the Dancehall from the early 1980s through the 1990s. A selected discography of the performer includes: "Them A Mad Over Me" (1982), "Bad Boy Skanking" (1982), "Live At Kilamanjaro" (1983), "King Yellowman" (1984), Walking Jewelry Store" (1985), "Girls Them Pet" (1986, "Party" (1991), and "Mi Hot" (1991). When confronted by the media, Yellowman said: "I never know why they call it slackness. I talk about sex. but it's just what happens behind closed doors. What I talk is reality."

In 1982, Yellowman was diagnosed with skin cancer. Doctors told him he had only three years to live. Following many surgeries, the entertainer's cancer went into remission and he returned touring. In 1986, the cancer returned to his jaw. Surgery completely disfigured Yellowman's face, but he changed his sex talk to socially and politically chatter. With his 1994 album, "Prayer," he turned spiritual. He was back on tours with his latest records, "New York" (2003) and "Round I" (2005). His shows have remained sold-out around the world.

U-Roy

Known as the Originator, U-Roy shook up the island with his unorthodox DJ banter. Although he was not the first Jamaican DJ to cut a record, Sir Lord Comic and King Stitt were in the vanguard of that genre. Born Ewart Beckford in Jamaica, in 1942, he got received his famous tag from a young family member unable to correctly pronounce his first name. The entertainer paid his dues with the Home Town Hi-Fi sound system established by King Tubby. U-Roy flopped in his early records. His first legit singles, "Dynamic Fashion Way" and "Earth's Rightful Rider," were engineered by two producers, Keith Hudson and Lee Perry, in separate projects in 1969. They didn't fly.

Treasure Isle Chief Duke Reid gave him a break and permitted him to "toast" or rap over a few instrumental tracks. In 1970, he took over the airwaves with three singles: "Wake The Town," "Rule The Nation," and "Wear You to the Ball." His 1971 debut album, "Version Galore," further secured his place in the music. Success didn't bring financial reward but he was determined to purpose his career. He worked with other producers who allowed him to expand his rich-voiced style of "toasting" over the rhythm, often timing his phrasing to the breaks of the music. Stretching the boundaries of the music, he performed with such artists as Joe Gibbs, Glen Brown, Niney Holness, and Lloyd Charmers.

U-Roy's rise to fame was slow, and took almost a decade. Lee Perry paired U-Roy with Peter Tosh and recorded "Selassie," a version of Ras Michael & the Sons of Negus' "Ethiopian National Anthem." He set up his own labels and even revived his career with projects by producer Prince Tony Robinson in the mid-1970s. Other records of U-Roy included: "U-Roy" (1974), "Dread in a Babylon" (1975), "Rasta Ambassador" (1977), "Jah Son of Africa" (1978), "Love Is Not a Gamble" (1980) and "Foundation Skank 1971-1975" (2009). Critical acclaim again found U-Roy with collaborations with Tappa Zukie in the late 1980s and UK's Mad professor in the 1990s.

Vintage and Modern Reggae Album Collection

Essential

Albums

Forward
The Abyssinians
(1982)

Satta Massagana
The Abyssinians
(1976)

Arise
The Abyssinians
(1978)

Declaration of Dub
The Abyssinians
(1998)

Satta Dub
The Abyssinians
(1998)

Guess Who's Coming To Dinner
Black Uhuru
(1981)

Rasta, Babylon, Jamming

Sinsemilla
Black Uhuru
(1980)

Anthem
Black Uhuru
(1984)

The Dub Factor
Black Uhuru
(1983)

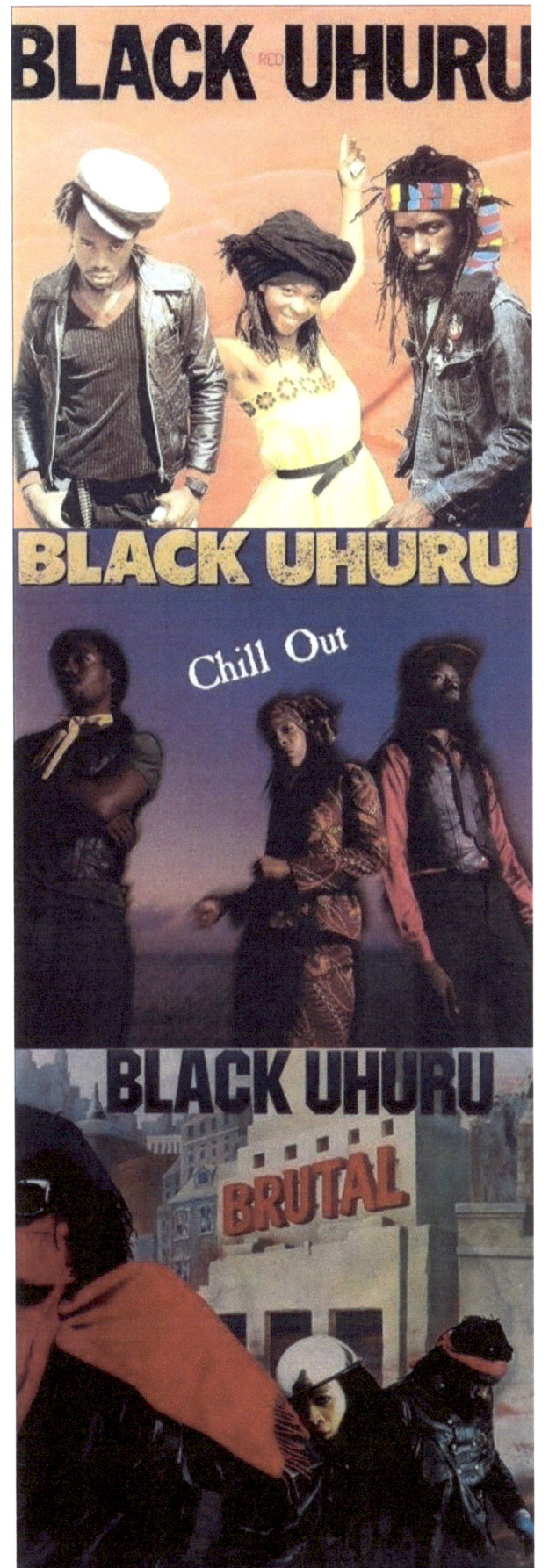

Red
Black Uhuru
(1981)

Chill Out
Black Uhuru
(1982)

Brutal
Black Uhuru
(1986)

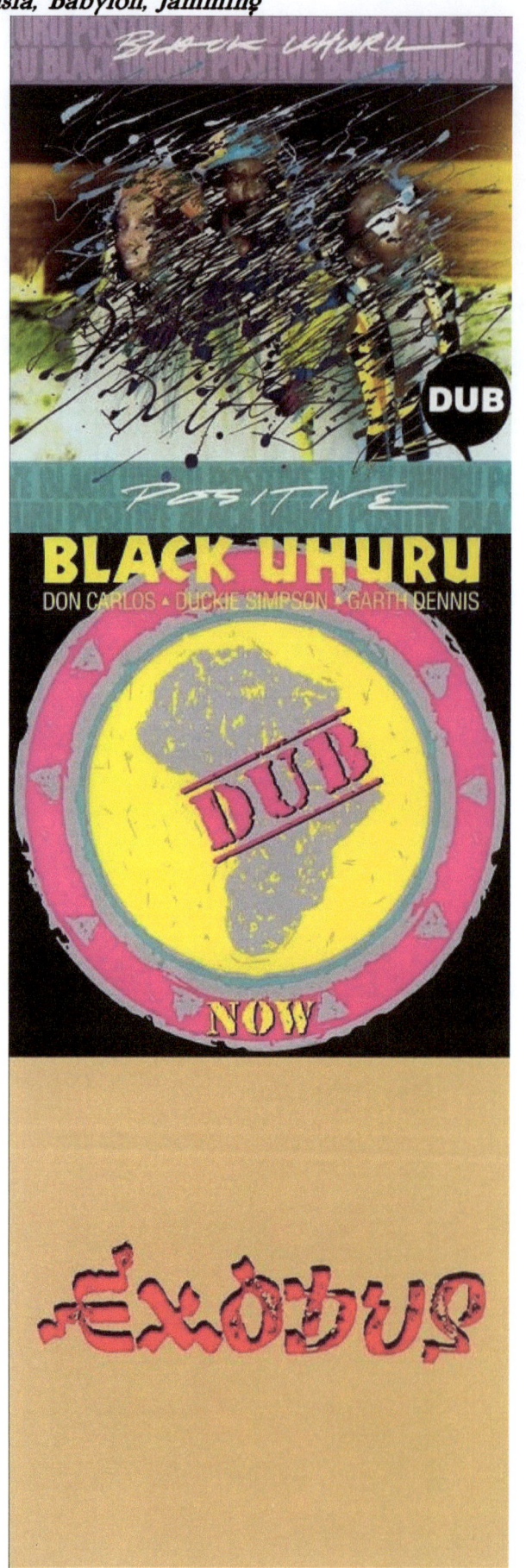

Positive Dub
Black Uhuru
(1987)

Now Dub
Black Uhuru
(1990)

Exodus
Bob Marley & the Wailers
(1977)

Robert Fleming

Kaya
Bob Marley & the Wailers
(1978)

Rastaman Vibration
Bob Marley & the Wailers
(1976)

Survival
Bob Marley & the Wailers
(1979)

Rasta, Babylon, Jamming

Uprising
Bob Marley & the Wailers
(1980)

**DUBD'SCO
Volumes 1 & 2**
Bunny Wailer
(1999)

Blackheart Man
Bunny Wailer
(1976)

68

Robert Fleming

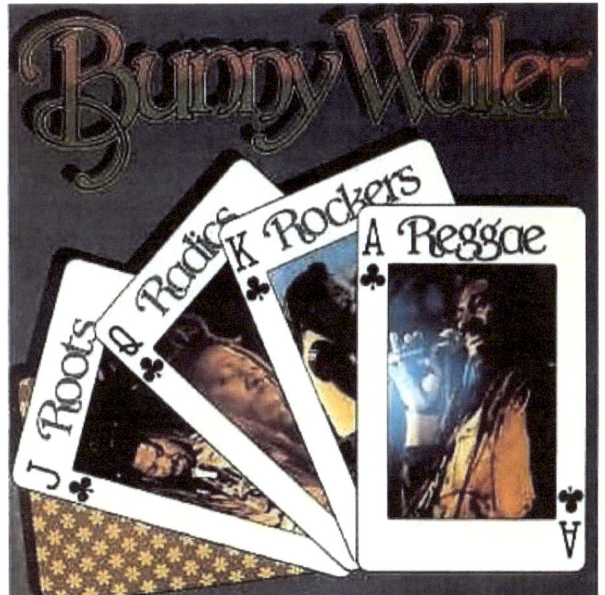

Roots, Radics, Rockers, Reggae
Bunny Wailer
(1987)

Protest
Bunny Wailer
(1987)

Voice of Jamaica
Buju Banton
(1993)

Rasta, Babylon, Jamming

Til Shiloh
Buju Banton
(1995)

Inna Heights
Buju Banton
(1997)

Man In The Hills
Burning Spear
(1976)

Robert Fleming

Social Living
Burning Spear
(1978)

Marcus Garvey
Burning Spear
(1975)

Garvey's Ghost
Burning Spear
(1976)

Rasta, Babylon, Jamming

HAIL H.I.M.
Burning Spear
(1980)

Live in Paris
Burning Spear
(1989)

The Fittest of the Fittest
Burning Spear
(1983)

Robert Fleming

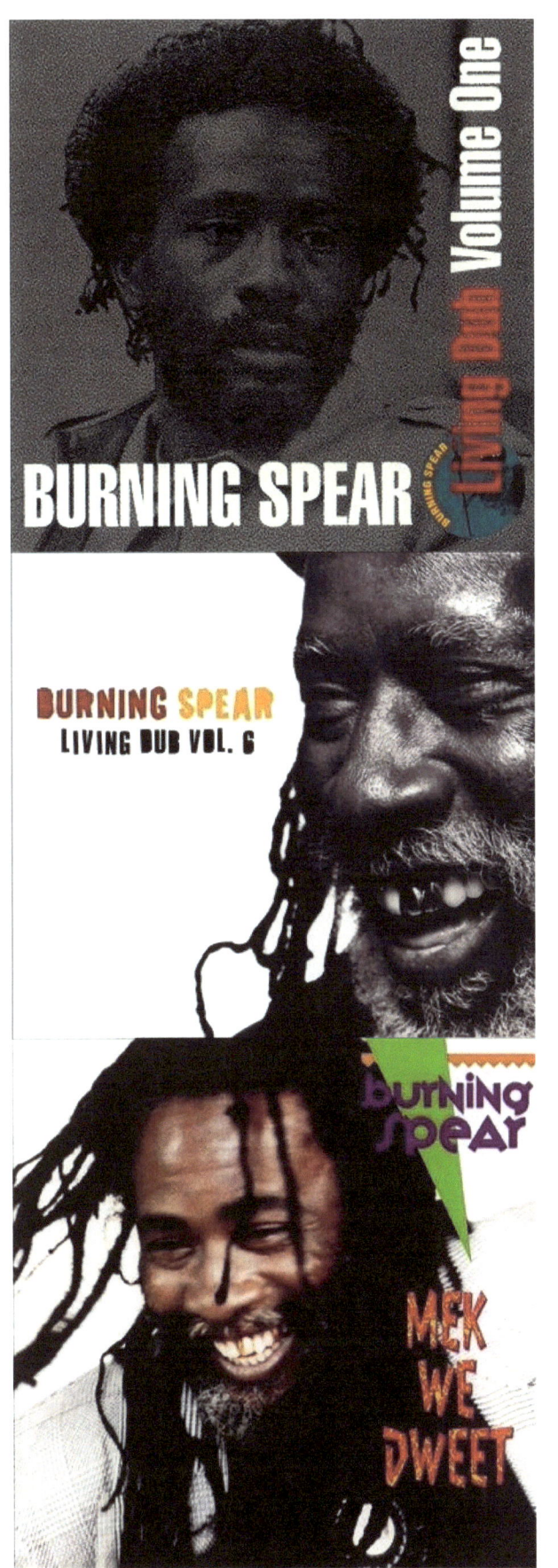

Living Dub Volume One
Burning Spear
(1993)

Living Dub Vol. 6
Burning Spear
(2008)

Meek We Dweet
Burning Spear
(1990)

Rasta, Babylon, Jamming

More Fire
Capleton
(2000)

Still Blazin
Capleton
(2002)

Reign of Fire
Capleton
(2004)

Robert Fleming

West Won Ridim
Capleton
(2004)

Two Sevens Clash
Culture
(1978)

Harder Than The Rest
Culture
(1978)

Rasta, Babylon, Jamming

Welcome to Jamrock
Damian (Jr. Gong) Marley
(2005)

The Master Has Come Back
Damian (Jr. Gong) Marley
(2005)

Words of Wisdom
Dennis Brown
(1979)

Robert Fleming

Money In My Pocket
Dennis Brown
(1983)

Wolves and Leopards
Dennis Brown
(1977)

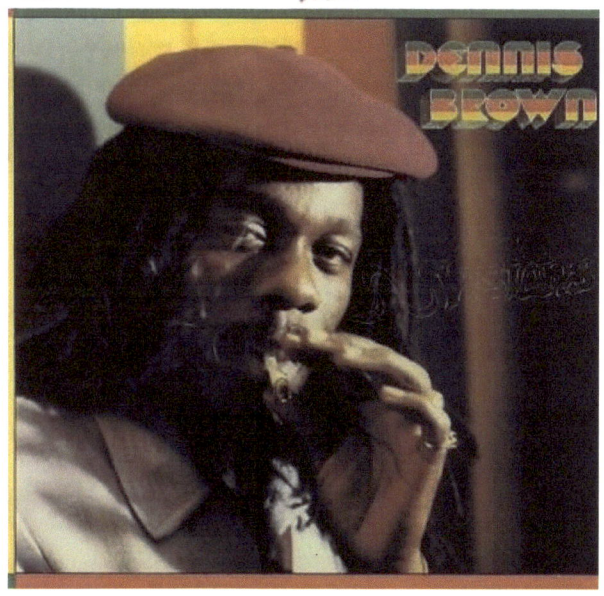

Visions
Dennis Brown
(1977)

Rasta, Babylon, Jamming

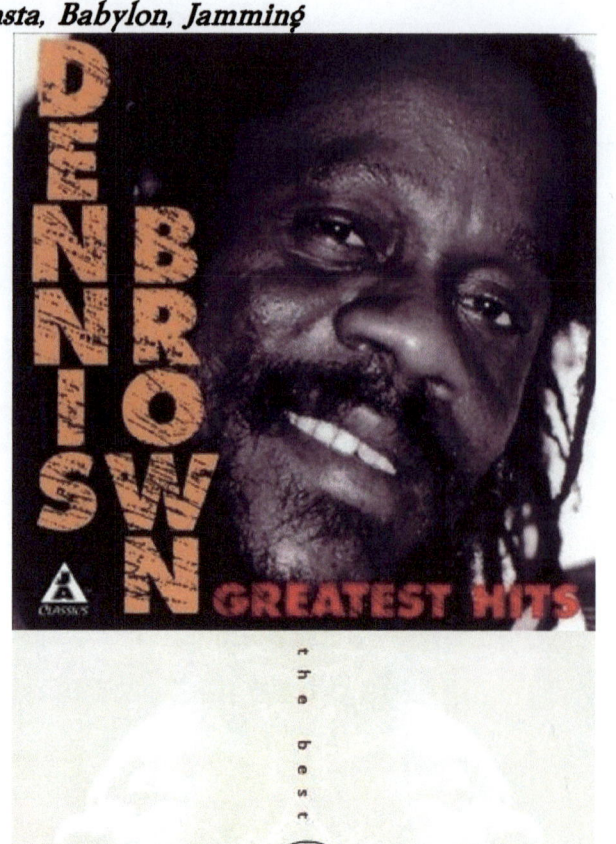

Greatests Hits
Dennis Brown
(1970s)

**Love & Hate
The Best of
Dennis Brown**
Dennis Brown
(1996)

Love Light
Dennis Brown
(1982)

Robert Fleming

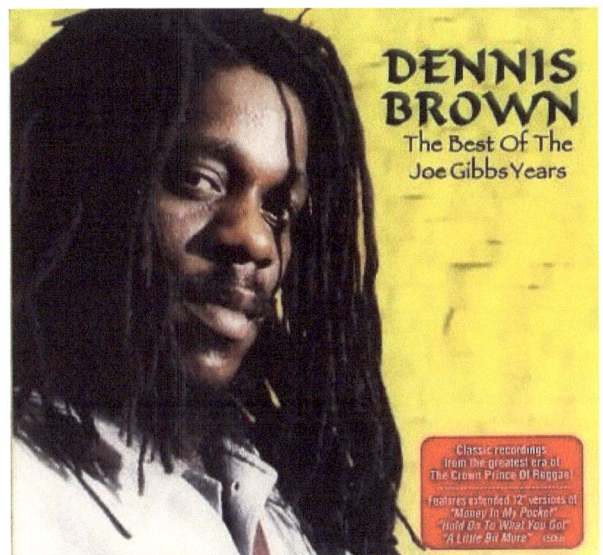

**The Best of the
Joe Gibbs Years**
Dennis Brown
2007)

Tuffer Than Stone
The Ethiopians
(1999)

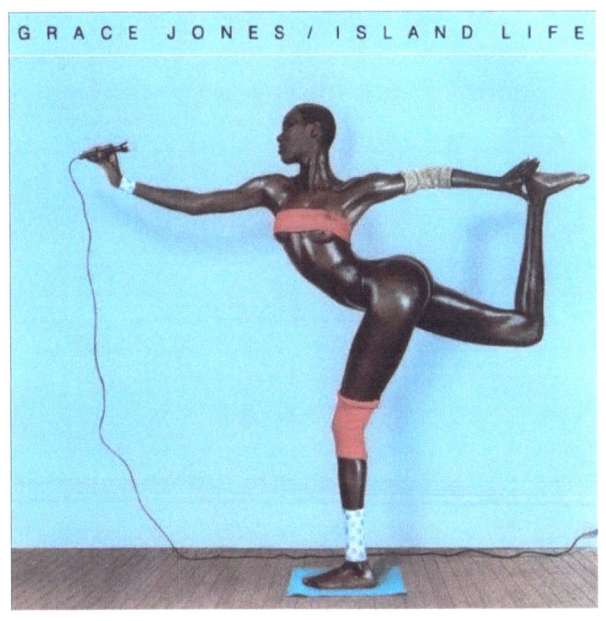

Island Life
Grace Jones
(1985)

Rasta, Babylon, Jamming

Night Nurse
Gregory Isaacs
(1982)

Cool Ruler
Gregory Isaacs
(1978)

Soon Forward
Gregory Isaacs
(1979)

More Gregory
Gregory Isaacs
(1981)

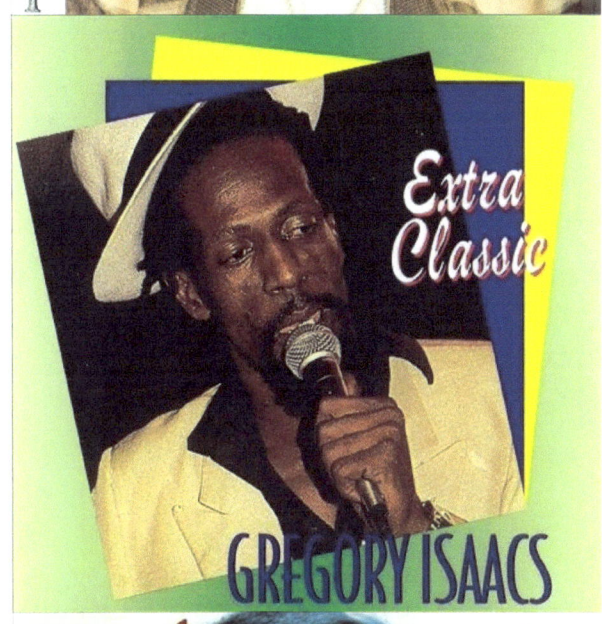

Extra Classic
Gregory Isaacs
(1977)

Mr. Isaacs
Gregory Isaacs
(1982)

Rasta, Babylon, Jamming

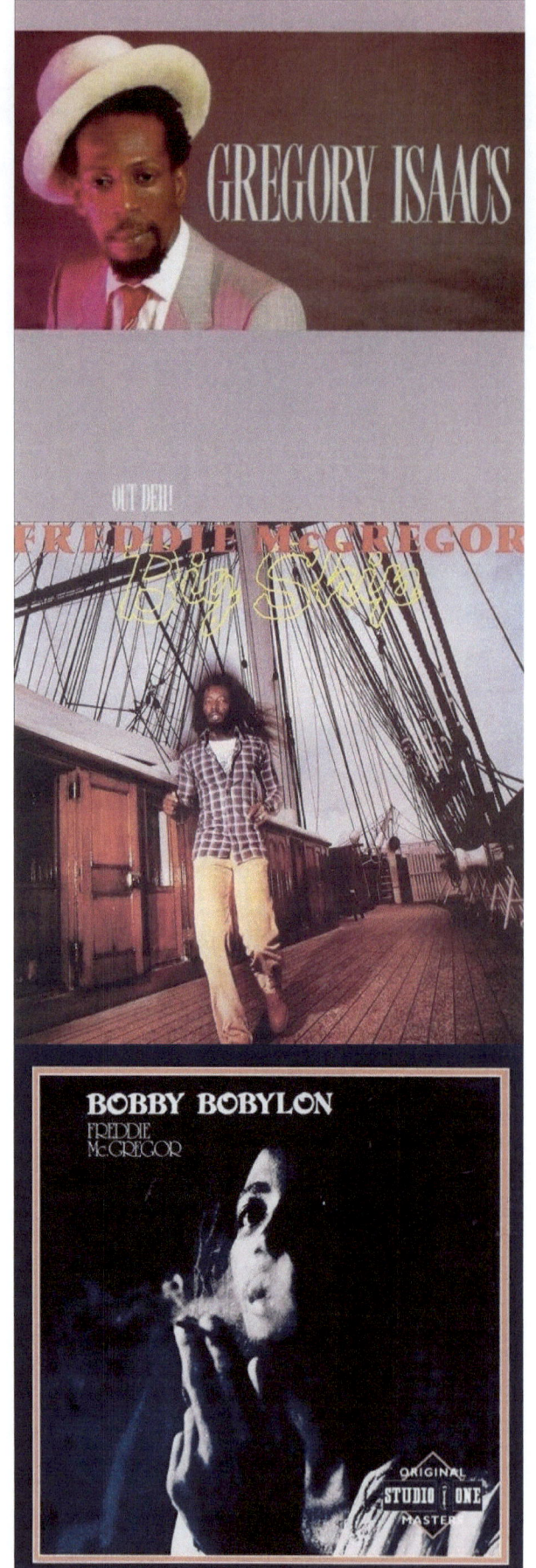

Out Deh!
Gregory Isaacs
(1983)

Big Ship
Freddie McGregor
(1982)

Bobby Bobylon
Freddie McGregor
(1980)

Robert Fleming

Come On Over
Freddie McGregor
(1984)

Across the Border
Freddie McGregor
(1984)

On Top
The Heptones
(1970)

Rasta, Babylon, Jamming

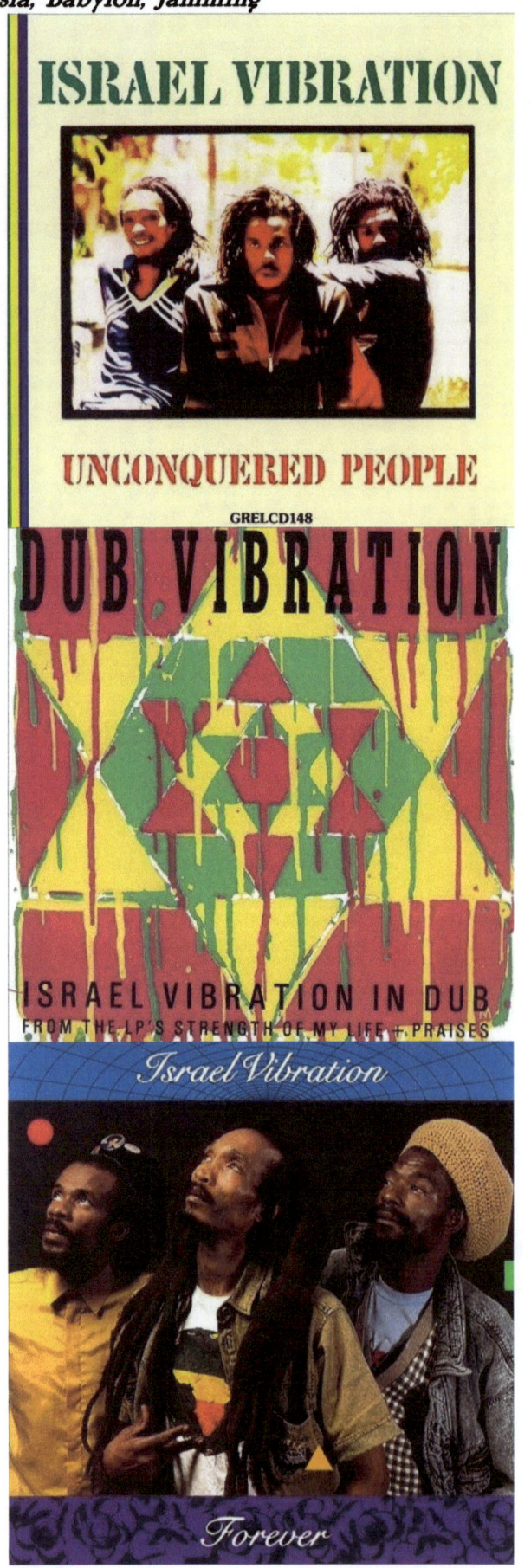

Unconquered People
Israel Vibration
(1980)

**Dub Vibration:
Israel Vibration in Dub**
Israel Vibration
(1990)

Forever
Israel Vibration
(1991)

Jimmy Cliff
Jimmy Cliff
(1969)

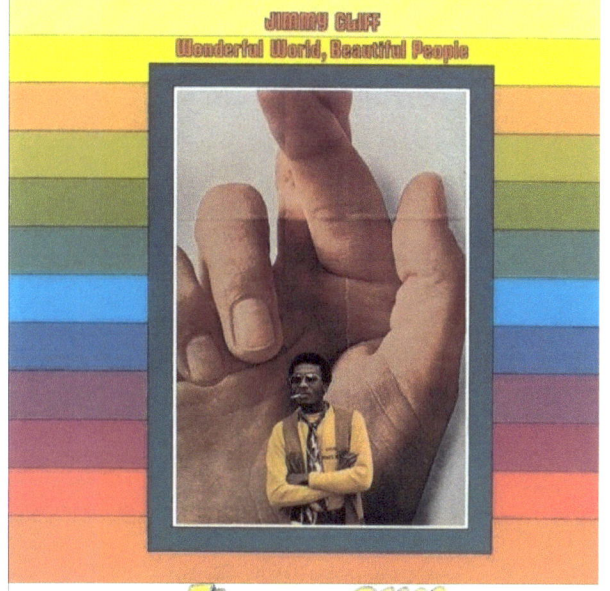

Wonderful World, Beautiful People
Jimmy Cliff
(1970)

The Harder They Come
Jimmy Cliff
(1972)

Rasta, Babylon, Jamming

A Love I Can Feel
John Holt
(1970)

Before the Next Tear Drop
John Holt
(1976)

Revolutionary Dream
Pablo Moses
(1976)

Robert Fleming

A Song
Pablo Moses
(1980)

We Refuse
Pablo Moses
(1990)

Legalize It
Peter Tosh
(1976)

Rasta, Babylon, Jamming

Bush Doctor
Peter Tosh
(1978)

Mama Africa
Peter Tosh
(1983)

Wanted Dread & Alive
Peter Tosh
(1981)

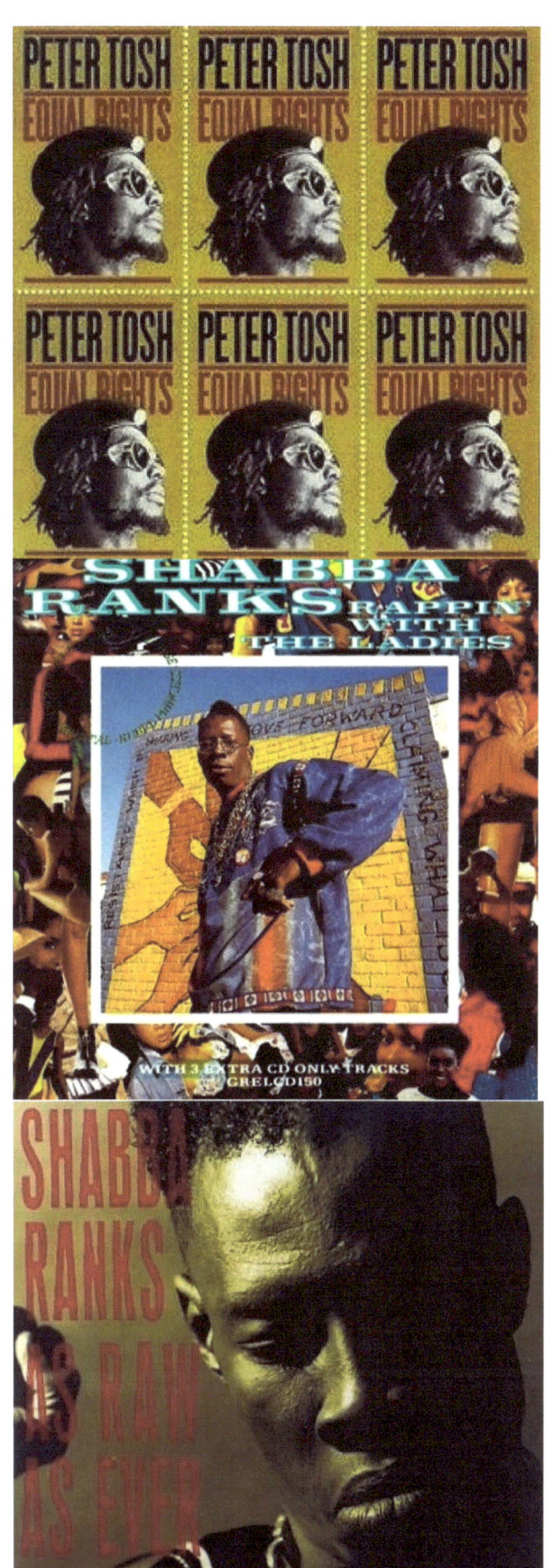

Equal Rights
Peter Tosh
(1977)

Rappin' With The Ladies
Shabba Ranks
(1988)

As Raw As Ever
Shabba Ranks
(1991)

Rasta, Babylon, Jamming

Boombastic
Shaggy
(1995)

Hotshot
Shaggy
(2000)

Handsworth Revolution
Steel Pulse
(1978)

Earth Crisis
Steel Pulse
(1984)

Rastafari Centennial Live in Paris
Steel Pulse
(1992)

Tribute to the Martyrs
Steel Pulse
(1979)

Rasta, Babylon, Jamming

True Democracy
Steel Pulse
(1982)

**Reggae Fever
Caught You**
Steel Pulse
(1980)

African Holocaust
Steel Pulse
(2004)

Robert Fleming

Rastanthology
Steel Pulse
(1996)

Third World
Third World
(1976)

96° In The Shade
Third World
(1977)

Rasta, Babylon, Jamming

Journey to Addis
Third World
(1978)

Rock the World
Third World
(1981)

You've Got the Power
Third World
(1982)

Robert Fleming

Dread in a Babylon
U Roy
(1975)

Rasta Ambassador
U Roy
(1977)

Natty Rebel
U Roy
(1976)

Rasta, Babylon, Jamming

16 Essential Reggae Films

1. **Reggae – 1970**

2. **The Harder They Come – 1973**

Rasta, Babylon, Jamming

3. **Rockers – 1978**

4. **Heartland Reggae – 1980**

5. **Countryman – 1982**

6. **Land of Look Behind – 1982**

7. **Dancehall Queen – 1997**

8. **Third World Cop – 1999**

9. **Shottas – 2002**

10. **Made in Jamaica - 2006**

11. **Jamdown – 2010**

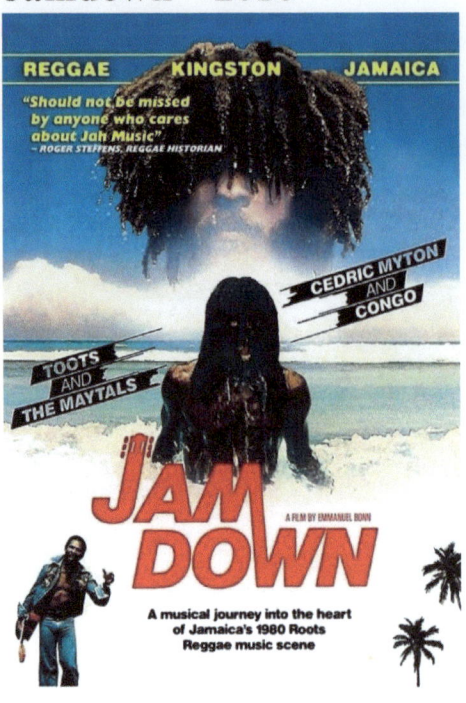

12. **Dreadlock Rock: The Story of Reggae Music – 2010**

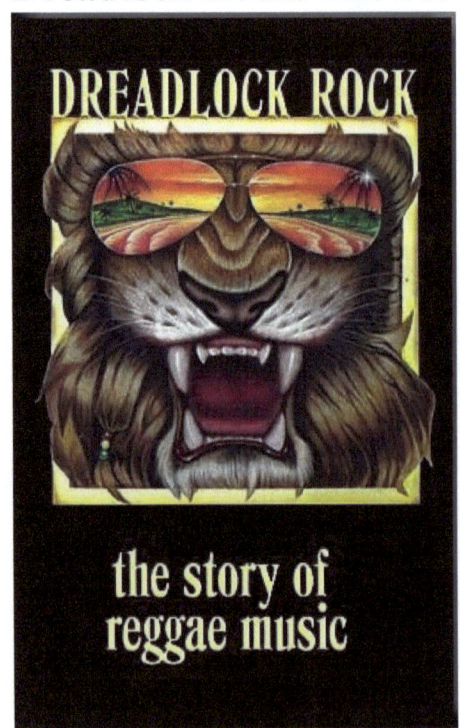

13. **Rocksteady: The Roots of Reggae – 2010**

14. **Awake Zion – 2014**

15. **Bob Marley: Giant – 2015**

16. **Reggae in a Babylon – 2015**

Selected Bibliography

Reggae Bloodlines: In Search Of The Music And Culture Of Jamaica – Stephen Davis and Peter Simon. DaCapo Press (1977)

Reggae: The Rough Guide – Steve Barlow and Peter Dalton. (1997)

This Is Reggae Music: The Story of Jamaica's Music – Lloyd Bradley. Grove Press (2000)

Reggae and Caribbean Music – Dave Thompson. Backbeat Books (2002)

I & I: The Natural Mystics: Marley, Tosh, and Wailer – Colin Grant. Jonathan Cape – London (2011)

Solid Foundation: An Oral History of Reggae - David Katz. Jawbone (2012)

The Encyclopedia of Reggae: The Golden Age of Roots Reggae – Mike Alleyne. Sterling (2012)

About the Authors

Robert Fleming, a freelance journalist and editor, formerly worked as a writer-consultant with ex CBS News President Fred Friendly, boss of the legendary Edward R. Morrow for PBS TV show, *Media and Society,* after graduating from Columbia University's Journalism School. Employed throughout 1980s and into 1990s, he served as a reporter for N.Y. Daily News, earning several honors including a N.Y. Press Club award and a Revson Fellowship in 1990. He worked as a freelance editor and book editor at Random House's imprint, One World. He taught courses in film and journalism at Manhattan's The New School His articles and reviews have appeared in the New York Times, Washington Post, U.S. News and World Report, Essence, Black Enterprise, Omni, Black Issues Book Review, Quarterly Black Review, and Publishers Weekly. His non-fiction books include *Rescuing A Neighborhood, The Success of Caroline Jones, The Wisdom of the Elders,* and *The African-American Writers Handbook.* His fiction consists *Fever In The Blood, Havoc After Dark, Gift of Faith, Gift of Truth,* and *Gift of Revelation.* He has edited four anthologies: *After Hours, Intimacy, Muntu Poets Anthology Vol. 2 – 47 Years Later with Russell* Atkins, and *Free Jazz: Creative Originality, Controlled Surprise.*

K Kelly McElroy. At the helm of Uptown Media Joint Ventures, K Kelly is following his passion of helping authors get their viable stories published and marketed to their readers! This passion includes expanding the audiences for recording artists and freelance journalists, as well!

K Kelly is an avid Modern Jazz enthusiast. He proudly owns a vintage collection of over 1000 classic jazz CDs. His first jazz book, a buying guide, *Best of the Best Modern Jazz* was an effort to compile his significant knowledge of the genre to assist others who want to develop and enjoy their own modern jazz collection. Modern jazz Classics expands on the concept by adding biographical information for key musicians of the modern jazz era.

K Kelly is a contributor to Robert Fleming's noted work *Free Jazz* and author of the book, *Modern Jazz Classics*, a concise, yet comprehensive, book on the best of modern jazz albums.

Rasta, Babylon, Jamming

The Music and Culture of Roots Reggae

ROBERT FLEMING

With K Kelly McElroy

www.ingramcontent.com/pod-product-compliance
Lightning Source LLC
Chambersburg PA
CBHW042032150426
43200CB00002B/20